The Emergence of British Parliamentary Democracy in the Nineteenth Century

MAJOR ISSUES IN HISTORY

Editor

C. WARREN HOLLISTER

University of California, Santa Barbara

William F. Church: *The Impact of Absolutism in France: National Experience under Richelieu, Mazarin, and Louis XIV*
Robert O. Collins: *The Partition of Africa: Illusion or Necessity*
J. B. Conacher: *The Emergence of Parliamentary Democracy in Britain in the Nineteenth Century*
Gerald D. Feldman: *German War Aims, 1914-1918: The Development of an Historical Debate*
Frank J. Frost: *Democracy and the Athenians*
Paul Hauben: *The Spanish Inquisition*
Bennett D. Hill: *Church and State in the Middle Ages*
Boyd H. Hill: *The Rise of the First Reich: Germany in the Tenth Century*
C. Warren Hollister: *The Impact of the Norman Conquest*
C. Warren Hollister: *The Twelfth-Century Renaissance*
Thomas M. Jones: *The Becket Controversy*
Tom B. Jones: *The Sumerian Problem*
Jeffry Kaplow: *France on the Eve of Revolution*
Archibald Lewis: *Islamic World and the West*
Anthony Molho: *Social and Economic Foundations of the Italian Renaissance*
E. W. Monter: *European Witchcraft*
Donald Queller: *The Latin Conquest of Constantinople*
Joachim Remak: *The First World War: Causes, Conduct, Consequences*
Jeffrey Russell: *Medieval Religious Dissent*
Max Salvadori: *European Liberalism*
Arthur J. Slavin: *Humanism, Reform, and Reformation*
W. Warren Wagar: *The Idea of Progress Since the Renaissance*
Bertie Wilkinson: *The Creation of the Medieval Parliament*
L. Pearce Williams: *Relativity Theory: Its Origins and Impact on Modern Thought*
Roger L. Williams: *The Commune of Paris, 1871*

The Emergence of British Parliamentary Democracy in the Nineteenth Century

*The Passing of the Reform Acts of
1832, 1867, and 1884–1885*

EDITED BY
J. B. Conacher

John Wiley and Sons, Inc. New York · London · Sydney · Toronto

Library of Congress Catalogue Card Number: 72-136711

Cloth: ISBN 0-471-16750-9
Paper: ISBN 0-471-16751-7

Printed in the United States of America

10   9   8   7   6   5   4   3   2   1

SERIES PREFACE

The reading program in a history survey course traditionally has consisted of a large two-volume textbook and, perhaps, a book of readings. This simple reading program requires few decisions and little imagination on the instructor's part, and tends to encourage in the student the virtue of careful memorization. Such programs are by no means things of the past, but they certainly do not represent the wave of the future.

The reading program in survey courses at many colleges and universities today is far more complex. At the risk of over-simplification, and allowing for many exceptions and overlaps, it can be divided into four categories: (1) textbook, (2) original source readings, (3) specialized historical essays and interpretive studies, and (4) historical problems.

After obtaining an overview of the course subject matter (textbook), sampling the original sources, and being exposed to selective examples of excellent modern historical writing (historical essays), the student can turn to the crucial task of weighing various possible interpretations of major historical issues. It is at this point that memory gives way to creative critical thought. The "problems approach," in other words, is the intellectual climax of a thoughtfully conceived reading program and is, indeed, the most characteristic of all approaches to historical pedagogy among the newer generation of college and university teachers.

The historical problems books currently available are many and varied. Why add to this information explosion? Because the Wiley Major Issues Series constitutes an endeavor to produce something new that will respond to pedagogical needs thus far unmet. First, it is a series of individual volumes—one per problem. Many good teachers would much prefer to select their own historical issues rather than be tied to an inflexible sequence of issues imposed by a publisher and bound together between two covers. Second, the Wiley Major Issues Series is based on the idea of approaching the significant problems of history through a deft interweaving of primary sources and secondary analysis, fused together by the skill of a scholar-editor. It is felt that the essence of a historical issue cannot be satisfactorily probed either by placing a body of undigested source materials into the hands of inexperienced students or by limiting these students to the controversial literature of modern scholars who debate the meaning of sources the student never sees. This series approaches historical problems by exposing students to both the finest historical thinking on the issue and some of the evidence on which this thinking is based. This synthetic approach should prove far more fruitful than either the raw-source approach or the exclusively second-hand approach, for it combines the advantages—and avoids the serious disadvantages—of both.

Finally, the editors of the individual volumes in the Major Issues Series have been chosen from among the ablest scholars in their fields. Rather than faceless referees, they are historians who know their issues from the inside and, in most instances, have themselves contributed significantly to the relevant scholarly literature. It has been the editorial policy of this series to permit the editor-scholars of the individual volumes the widest possible latitude both in formulating their topics and in organizing their materials. Their scholarly competence has been unquestioningly respected; they have been encouraged to approach the problems as they see fit. The titles and themes of the series volumes have been suggested in nearly every case by the scholar-editors themselves. The criteria have been (1) that the issue be of relevance to undergraduate lecture courses in history, and (2) that it be an issue which the scholar-editor knows thoroughly and in which he has done creative work. And, in general, the second criterion has been given precedence over the first. In short, the question "What are the significant historical issues today?" has been answered not by general editors or sales departments but by the scholar-teachers who are responsible for these volumes.

University of California,   *C. Warren Hollister*
Santa Barbara

PREFACE

The Reform Acts of 1832, 1867, and 1884–1885 are important milestones in the emergence of parliamentary democracy in Great Britain. The limits of space make it impossible to go beyond the passage of these acts in the readings since the full story embraces much of British history of the past two centuries; but it is hoped that the reader's appetite will be whetted to follow the story further on his own. Some additional reading suggestions are included in the bibliography.

The readings that follow are, of course, a tiny fraction of the vast mass of primary and secondary sources available in print on the Reform Acts of 1832, 1867, and 1884–1885. They are selected by way of example and, in the case of the original sources, with a view to giving the atmosphere and some idea of the range of debate. The statutes themselves seemed too long and technical for a selection of readings of this sort. They will be conveniently found with some minor deletions in W. C. Costin and J. Steven Watson, *The Law and Working of the Constitution*, Vol. II (London, 1952).

It will be understood that the selections from *Hansard* represent only a small proportion of the total speakers in any debate and that in most cases only a small part of any single speech. The deletion marks (. . .) sometimes indicate brief and sometimes quite lengthy omissions, but the latter case may generally be determined from the column numbers in the references. (*Hansard* is numbered by columns, not by pages, and all references to it are to the third series.)

Since most of the readings are from much longer books, articles, speeches, etc., I have not started or ended an extract with deletion marks (. . .) unless it begins or ends in the middle of a paragraph. In the readings from secondary sources I have had to cut out most of the notes for lack of space, but the books themselves can easily be consulted by students wishing to see the sources. I have added a few notes of my own to identify some individuals not mentioned in the introductions.

The three introductions are conceived primarily as guides to the readings to help the reader thread his way through the maze of events which led to the passage of each of the Reform Acts. Editorial comment is kept to the minimum, since the significance of each of the acts is discussed in the various selections from secondary authorities.

J. B. Conacher
University of Toronto

CONTENTS

PART I

The First Reform Act of 1832

PART II

The Second Reform Act of 1867

PART III

The Third Reform Act of 1884 and the Redistribution Act of 1885

The Emergence of British
Parliamentary Democracy
in the Nineteenth Century

PART I

The First Reform Act of 1832

INTRODUCTION

Among the representative institutions that appeared in Western Europe in the later Middle Ages the English Parliament was unique, not only because it survived but because over the centuries it grew in power and prestige. In the reign of Edward I (1272–1307) the expedient was adopted of calling elected representatives of the counties and the towns or boroughs to the King's Great Council, or Parliament, to obtain the assent of the lesser landowners and burghers to the levying of taxes required to meet the ever-growing expenses of royal wars. In the course of time these elected representatives took to sitting separately from the peers in their "House of Commons," and by the later sixteenth century election as a member of Parliament was regarded as an honour rather than a burden, as it had appeared to be originally. Moreover, the role of Parliament in the making of statute law had now become fully established, and consequently it was in the interests of the crown to ensure a friendly majority in the popular house. Taking advantage of the new ambitions of the gentry for membership in the Commons, the Tudors and Stuarts created many new parliamentary boroughs, in most cases no longer because of their wealth and population but rather as convenient means of strengthening the parliamentary support of the Crown. Over 200 such seats were created in the sixteenth and seventeenth centuries, while the Act of Union with Scotland added 45 more and the Irish Union another hundred, which brought the total to 658.

During the period of the Puritan rebellion (1642–1660), consideration was given to reforming the anomalies that had crept into the parliamentary system and to ways of making it more representative. All such ideas, however, were swept away with the restoration of the Stuart monarchy in 1660. The place of Parliament in the constitution was enhanced by the Revolution of 1688, but the settlement that followed that revolution froze the pattern of parliamentary representation. Indeed, from the Septennial Act of 1716, which fixed

3

the maximum life of a parliament at seven years, there was no further formal change in the framework of Parliament (apart from the addition of Irish seats by the Act of Union of 1800) until the passing of the Great Reform Bill in 1832. This long period of quiescence represented a reaction to the traumatic experience of the seventeenth-century revolutions, but it also marked the triumphant ascendancy of the landed classes who found the unreformed Parliament an ideal means of perpetuating their rule.

Inevitably, however, as the country became more prosperous and secure, some men began to see the imperfections in the parliamentary system that had been complacently pronounced perfect. First of all the Radicals of Middlesex and then the electors of Yorkshire raised the cry for reform, and spokesmen appeared in Parliament itself. The first comprehensive parliamentary motion for an extension of the franchise and a redistribution of seats was made in 1776 by the Radical member for Middlesex, John Wilkes (1727–1797). The cause was taken up by no less a person than the younger Pitt (1759–1806), who introduced motions when out of office in 1782 and 1783 and again while Prime Minister in 1785, but with no success.

The French Revolution initially gave a stimulus to the forces for reform, but a reaction quickly set in as the Terror spread in France and Britain went to war with the revolutionary government. Never-theless, under the leadership of Charles James Fox (1749–1806), the rump of the Whig party, which was left in opposition to the reactionary wartime government of Pitt, continued to pay at least lip service to the cause of parliamentary reform. In 1793 and 1797 Fox's young lieutenant, the aristocratic Charles Grey (1764–1845), defiantly introduced further reform motions, but against overwhelm-ing opposition.

Although Grey succeeded Fox as leader of the Whigs on the latter's death in 1806, he soon inherited his father's seat in the House of Lords, where his zeal in the cause of Reform seemed to languish. How-ever, in the next generation of Whigs that entered Parliament in the years following the peace settlement of 1815, new spokesmen were to be found, in particular Grey's son-in-law, John Lambton, (1792–1840), the future Lord Durham, and Lord John Russell (1792–1878), scion of the Whig house of Bedford. Both men made a series of reform proposals during these years, but the issue remained an open one in the party, treated coolly by some of the old aristocracy, but strongly demanded by the small Radical group nicknamed "the Mountain" that had appeared in the Commons. Outside Parliament the demand for parliamentary reform, largely muted during the war, became vocal and widespread with the formation of Hampden Clubs and political unions, and great public meetings were held under the diverse leadership of such men as the old-fashioned Radical M.P. Sir Francis Burdett (1770–1844), the veteran Reform champions Major Cartwright (1740–1824) and Christopher Wyvill (1740–1822), the popular journalist William Cobbett (1762–1835), and "Orator" Hunt (1773–1835), the professional demagogue. Eleven people were killed in the "Peterloo Massacre" of 1819, when the local authorities at Manchester broke up a quiet reform demonstration at St. Peter's field, where more than 50,000 people had gathered to hear Hunt speak.

Nevertheless, as long as the Whigs remained in opposition the cause of reform looked hopeless and the Tory heirs of the younger Pitt seemed to be in office permanently. Actually their position was less secure than it appeared to be on the surface. The administrative reforms of the previous half-century had greatly reduced the patronage available to the King's ministers, and this had been the cement that held together all eighteenth-century administrations. Moreover, the Tory successors of Lord Liverpool (1770–1827), who had been Prime Minister from 1812 to 1827, lacked his flair for keeping together the diverse elements which made up the loosely knit second Tory party. In particular, the Duke of Wellington (1769–1852) had antagonized the strongly Protestant "ultra" Tories by his surrender to Daniel O'Connell (1775–1847) on the issue of Catholic emancipation. Some of these even began to think that a more representative House of Commons would be a more English and Protestant one and consequently that a reformed House of Commons would not have passed Catholic emancipation! The defection of some of these ultra Tories helped to precipitate Wellington's downfall in November of 1830.

The death of George IV in 1830 and the accession of William IV, his brother, necessitated a general election that summer. Despite the anxious calculations of the Government whips, Wellington failed to secure enough support to sustain his government in the new Parliament (by eighteenth-century standards an almost unprecedented situation). Whig candidates supported the growing public demand for reform in the election, and when Parliament met in the autumn, Lord Grey pressed the matter in the House of Lords. By his categorical statement denying the need for reform, Wellington drove the final nail into his own political coffin. The public, stimulated by the success of the moderate July Revolution in France, were loud in their indignation. On 15 November the government was defeated in the House of Commons by a majority of twenty-nine, with some sixty supposed supporters joining the Opposition.

Wellington immediately resigned and the King did not hesitate to call on Grey to form a new government. It was inevitably committed to parliamentary reform, as was attested by the inclusion of Durham and Russell in the ministry (although Russell was initially left outside the Cabinet) as well as Henry Brougham (1778–1868), a one-time Radical reformer, who became Lord Chancellor. Significantly the new government contained four Canningites or Liberal Tories, including Lords Palmerston (1784–1865) and Melbourne (1782–1853), and one ultra Tory, the Duke of Richmond (1791–1860), who were all estranged from Wellington and prepared to accept a reform bill.

"His administration formed," Professor Butler has written, "it was Lord Grey's chief duty . . . to approach what he himself called 'the perilous question' of reform. . . . Hating to be hustled he would gladly have postponed the question; only cruel necessity compelled its discussion in the heat and glare of popular excitement."[1] Initially he was inclined to propose a limited measure; "but after full consideration and discussing the matter with his colleagues [in the words of his statement in Parliament], he was convinced that nothing short of the present measure would tend to the desired result of satisfying the country."[2] He was undoubtedly influenced by his Radical son-in-law, Lord Durham, and the latter's appointment as chairman of the Cabinet committee to draft the bill was clearly all important.[3] Grey was an opportunist in Butler's view and was anxious to obtain a "permanent solution." To this end he was ready to accept "a really extensive measure."

The committee brought in much wider proposals than their colleagues had anticipated, including the elimination of 168 seats and the extension of the vote to all ratepaying householders paying £10 annual rent in the boroughs. Except for the ballot, the committee's proposals obtained the warm support of Grey and were accepted.[4]

The House of Commons was even more surprised at the extent of the bill, which was presented by Lord John Russell on 1 March 1831,[5]

[1] J. R. M. Butler, *The Passing of the Great Reform Bill*, p. 157.
[2] *Ibid.*
[3] See No. 1. p. 11.
[4] See No. 2. p. 13.
[5] See Nos. 3A and B and 4A, pp. 16, 17 and 18.

and it only passed its second reading (the debate on principle) by a majority of one. The most effective spokesman for the bill proved to be the young T. B. Macaulay (1800–1859), the great Whig historian and essayist, who had only recently arrived in the House, where he quickly made his reputation as an orator.[6] Defeat on an amendment in committee, moved by General Gascoyne, led to the dissolution of Parliament by the King on the recommendation of the ministers.[7] A second election greatly increased the government's majority, owing to the unprecedented wave of public opinion in favor of the bill, opinion that affected candidates normally immune to such pressure.

When the new Parliament met in June, a second reform bill was introduced with only changes in detail. After further long debate it passed its third reading in the Commons in September with one opposition amendment accepted by the government, the famous Chandos clause, which extended the county franchise to £50 tenants-at-will (i.e., farmers without leases, paying at least £50 annual rent); this was technically an extension of the suffrage meeting Radical approval, but actually it was an extension of the political influence of the landlords as long as there was no secret ballot. All this time there was mounting agitation out of doors from a public growing impatient at the long delays and when, after a great debate in the House of Lords, the bill was defeated on its second reading on the night of October 7–8 by a majority of 41,[8] public indignation was intense. Serious riots with loss of life and property broke out in Derby, Nottingham, and Bristol. New political unions sprang up throughout the country and their activity increased throughout the autumn. It was in this area that the influence of the Benthamite Radicals was greatest, in particular James Mill (1773–1854), Bentham's closest and most influential disciple; Joseph Parkes (1796–1865), a Birmingham solicitor and later chief Liberal party agent; and Francis Place (1771–1854), a London tailor and key organizer of the Radical Westminster election committee. These three men and some of their associates, such as the banker George Grote, had important contacts with some of the ministers or their secretaries, with various newspaper editors, and with businessmen in the City of London, all of which they systematically exploited to the utmost.[9]

[6]See No. 4B, p. 24.

[7]See No. 5, p. 33.

[8]See Nos. 6A, B, and C, pp. 36, 37 and 38.

[9]It is regretted that it is not possible to include an extract from J. Hamburger *James Mill and the Art of Revolution* (New Haven, 1963), where this story is fully told.

After negotiating with some moderate Tory peers, known as "the Waverers," who were anxious to avoid a crisis, the Cabinet decided to try again with a third bill. This made some modifications in the disfranchising and enfranchising schedules that met some of the opposition objections without surrendering on either the principle or scope of the measure. The extent of the public furor led the ministers to recall Parliament in December and introduce their third bill earlier than they had intended. While the bill was still in the Commons, the Cabinet sought to obtain assurances from the King that he would appoint a sufficient number of peers, if it became necessary, to guarantee the passage of this bill through the House of Lords,[10] but they decided against any early token appointments for fear of antagonizing the Waverers in the Lords, on whose support they were now counting for the crucial second reading. In January the King gave the necessary assurance,[11] but by the end of March, after the bill had finally passed its third reading in the Commons, he was beginning to change his mind and show hostility as a result of pressure from his family and members of the court. On 13–14 April the bill passed its second reading in the House of Lords, but on 7 May a hostile procedural amendment went against the government. Lord Grey consequently asked the King to fulfill his promise and appoint a sufficient number of peers to ensure the bill's continued passage in the Lords.[12] The King, despite his earlier assurances, now had a change of heart and refused the request.[13]

Lord Grey resigned on 9 May and the King called on the Duke of Wellington to form a government. These events led the House of Commons to pass a motion introduced by Lord Ebrington, urging the King not to appoint any ministers who were not prepared to carry the bill into effect. The ensuing nine days, the famous "Days of May," were a period of tense suspense and tremendous public excitement. The whole country seemed to concentrate its attention on the crisis, which received maximum attention in a predominantly proreform press. The political unions redoubled their activities, large public meetings were held everywhere, the working classes demonstrated their support for this largely middle-class cause, reform leaders in the provinces worked closely with those in London, and plans were laid

[10] See No. 7A, p. 39.
[11] See Nos. 7B and 7C, pp. 41 and 43.
[12] See No. 8A, p. 45.
[13] See No. 8B, p. 46.

to engineer a run on the banks.[14] Wellington was perhaps less impressed by these developments than might have been supposed, but Sir Robert Peel (1788–1850), the Tory leader in the Commons, refused to join a government to pass a Tory reform bill (as the King wanted), and so the Duke was forced to abandon the attempt. Grey returned to office and on 18 May, after two more anxious days of negotiation, the King agreed to undertake the creation of a sufficient number of peers to force the bill through the upper house as soon as it became necessary.[15] The mere announcement of this news was sufficient to overcome the opposition of the majority of the Tory peers, and on 4 June the bill passed its third and final reading in the Lords by a vote of 106 to 22.

It is difficult to say to what extent the public agitation and especially the threatened run on the banks were responsible for the solution of the crisis. A recent writer has suggested that the supposed danger of revolution was exaggerated,[16] but this was by no means clear at the time. In Professor Hamburger's view it was the deliberate intention of Mill and his friends to make the ministers suppose that the danger was greater than it was. "The emphasis was placed on appearances," he writes (p. 51). "The professional reformer, like the public relations man, dealt in images, and in his role as tactician, reality was his concern only in so far as it was necessary to shape it to give plausibility to the image he was trying to create." As with most human events the result was produced by a large number of interrelated factors of varying but indeterminate weight. The conscious or subconscious fear of revolution was undoubtedly a not unimportant element in the situation, but it was inextricably mixed up with a variety of political and personal considerations involving the King, his ministers, and other political leaders concerned.

The Reform Act of 1832 reformed both the franchise and the distribution of seats in the House of Commons. The total number of voters was doubled by the extension of the franchise in boroughs to householders who paid £10 rent annually and in the counties to tenants-at-will who paid £50 annual rent, as well as to a small number of leaseholders and copyholders, but many anomalies remained.[17] Even more important was the total disfranchisement of 56 and the

---

[14] See No. 8E, p. 49.

[15] See Nos. 8C and D, pp. 46 and 48.

[16] See J. Hamburger, *James Mill and the Art of Revolution*, pp. 100–110.

[17] There was no uniform borough franchise prior to 1832. "Ancient right" voters retained the franchise only if they fulfilled the new residence qualifications.

partial disfranchisement of 31 boroughs, mostly in the south, which made possible the redistribution of 143 seats. Sixty-five of these were distributed among new English boroughs to give representation to places, some of them large cities such as Manchester and Birmingham, hitherto unrepresented, and to increase the representation of the London metropolitan area; another 65 were distributed among the English counties, which were still underrepresented, and 13 were transferred from England to Scotland and Ireland.[18] The overrepresentation of the agricultural south of England was much reduced but not eliminated.

In this way the completely rotten boroughs, where the member was the mere nominee of the borough owner, were eliminated, but as Professor Gash[19] has demonstrated, more of the old system of influence remained than the Whig Liberal historians of earlier generations recognized.[20] Of the 187 English parliamentary boroughs, 123 had less than 1,000 electors, and of these 31 had not more than 300.[21] Owing to registration difficulties the increase in the electorate was less than anticipated. In 1832 it rose from something less than 500,000 to 813,000 (including many plural voters), or one-thirtieth of the population of the United Kingdom. In terms of the adult male population, however, this produced a ratio of 1 to 7 in the United Kingdom as a whole, but 1 to 5 in England and Wales as compared with 1 to 8 in Scotland and 1 to 20 in Ireland.[22] The new voters were drawn mainly from the middle class, for few workingmen outside London as yet paid £10 rent a year.

The Reform Act of 1832 was clearly not a democratic measure. The landed classes continued to dominate the House of Commons and to hold most of the high offices,[23] but there were important changes. Indeed, the purpose of the Reform Act had been, in Professor Gash's words, to destroy "the illegitimate and not the legitimate influence of property".[24] The elimination of the com-

---

[18] See No. 4A for the regional proposals.

[19] See No. 9C, p. 58.

[20] See also Norman Gash, *Politics in the Age of Peel* (London, 1953), Appendix D, pp. 438–439.

[21] *Ibid.*, p. 77.

[22] *Ibid.*, pp. 88–89.

[23] Professor D. C. Moore has argued that the Reform Act was less a blow against the power of the aristocracy than "against the powers of the ministers" ["The Other Face of Reform", *Victorian Studies*, V (1961), p. 34].

[24] Gash, *Politics in the Age of Peel*, p. 185.

pletely closed or rotten boroughs and the moderate extension of the franchise made more members of Parliament susceptible to public opinion than in the past, and in the larger boroughs candidates were often forced to make pledges to the electors and to take up causes, like free trade, that they might otherwise have ignored. At the same time the increase in the number of voters in most constituencies and the new registration requirements necessitated a greater degree of party organization. Better electoral organization was a factor in the return of the Tories, now called Conservatives, to office in 1841.

The passage of the First Reform Act also had important constitutional consequences affecting the Crown and both houses of Parliament. It soon became apparent, as Peel had warned in the debates, that the Crown would be unable to change ministers without deferring to the wishes of the Commons. The prime responsibility of the ministers was now to the House of Commons and the resultant development in cabinet government was first brilliantly described by Walter Bagehot (1826–1877) in his *English Constitution*, first published on the eve of the Second Reform Act of 1867. While the power of the Commons was enhanced, that of the Lords declined. Not only had many individual peers lost control of seats in the House of Commons, but, more seriously, the prestige and potential power of the upper house had suffered from the fact that it had been forced by the threatened creation of peers to accept a bill it had previously rejected. What had been done once could be done again, and a House of Commons bent on Reform would not be stopped. Actually in 1867 there was no issue between the two houses and in 1884 differences were reconciled by more peaceful means, but after 1832 the House of Lords could not ignore public opinion as it had done prior to the passing of the Great Reform Bill.

1   *The Cabinet Committee on Reform as Recalled by*
Sir James Graham

From the first formation of his Government he [Lord Grey] never ceased to contemplate the redemption of his pledge that a large and efficient measure of Parliamentary Reform should be proposed by him as Minister; and when he nominated the Committee to which

SOURCE. C. S. Parker, *Life and Letters of Sir James Graham* (London, 1907), Vol. I, pp. 119–121.

the framing of the first draft of the measure was confided, he selected
Lord Durham, his son-in-law, who enjoyed his confidence, and who
had known for years his private views and opinions on the subject; he
named Lord John Russell, who, like Lord Durham, had in Opposition
brought the question before Parliament, and who enjoyed with the
popular party a rising reputation; he added Lord Duncannon[1] on
account of his acquaintance with borough history and details, more
especially in Ireland; and I was considered not unworthy of a place in
that Committee because my zeal for Reform was supposed to exceed
the standard measure of the Whigs, because the Radicals did not
regard me with disfavour, and because my intimacy with Lord Durham
and with Lord John Russell ensured our cordial co-operation and
union.

The instructions of Lord Grey to this Committee, with the full
consent of his Cabinet, were, that the outline of a measure should be
prepared, large enough to satisfy public opinion and to afford sure
ground of resistance to further innovation, yet so based on property,
and on existing franchises and territorial divisions, as to run no risk
of overthrowing the form of Government which we desired only to
amend.

Such were the instructions of Lord Grey, and such were the wishes
and intentions of the leading members of the Administration.

The Committee met frequently, and discussed in the most amicable
manner first the principles and then the details of the scheme of
Reform which was ultimately submitted to the Cabinet. Lord Durham
held the pen, and committed to writing from time to time the points
which were fixed by our agreement; Lord John Russell furnished the
materials on which Schedules A and B were framed; the metropolitan
subdivision of the representation was pressed by Lord Durham; the
enlargement of the right of voting in towns was felt at once by all to
be indispensable. The freemen were hopelessly corrupt, and a franchise
resting on annual rent, and on the payment of rates and taxes, was by
common consent soon admitted to be the remedy.

In the first draft of the measure which we presented to the Cabinet
the annual value, if I mistake not, was £15 or £20, not £10. But it has
transpired that in this draft it was also proposed that votes should be
given secretly by ballot; and when, after full discussion in the Cabinet,
this suggestion of Ballot, which was made by the Committee *ad*

---

[1] John Ponsonby (1781–1847), Viscount Duncannon, later became fourth Earl
of Bessborough.

referendum, had been rejected, the value by way of compromise was reduced from £15 [£20] to £10.

No Bill was drawn until the consent of the King and of the Cabinet had been obtained to the plan of the Committee, with modifications. That plan was detailed in writing by Lord Durham, who reported on behalf of the Committee, in a paper drawn by him and settled by us, wherein we sustained by reasoning the form and the extent of our proposals, and endeavoured to show that the plan was in unison with the instructions of Lord Grey; that it was no bit by bit Reform; that it ought to satisfy, both by what it destroyed and by what it created; that it was safe in itself, and still more so as a tower of strength in covering future resistance to dangerous projects of ulterior change.

The measure therefore must be regarded as the fruit of Lord Grey's instructions to the Committee; as the compound of the deliberations and of the suggestions of the members composing that Committee, and as the ultimate compromise of the various opinions in the Cabinet, with whom the final decision rested.

2   *Report of the Cabinet Committee on Reform,*

January, 1831

In compliance with your directions, we have carefully examined into the state of the Representation, with a view to its thorough and effective Reform, and we now present to you, as the result of our labours, three Bills, amending the Representation of England, Scotland, and Ireland.

In framing them we have been actuated by the belief, that it is not the wish, or intention, of His Majesty's Ministers to concede only as much as might for the moment evade or stifle the general demand for a complete alteration of the existing system, or to propose the adoption of such a measure as could merely be considered a bare redemption of their pledges to their Sovereign and the country.

We have been, on the contrary, convinced that it is their desire to effect such a permanent settlement of this great and important question, as will no longer render its agitation subservient to the

SOURCE. Henry Earl Grey, ed., *The Reform Act, 1832; Correspondence of the Late Earl Grey with William IV, 1830–1832* (London, 1867), Vol. I, Appendix A, pp. 461–463.

designs of the factious and discontented; but by its wise and comprehensive provisions inspire all classes of the community with a conviction, that their rights and privileges are at length duly secured and consolidated.

We have not been insensible to the great and appalling dangers which attend any further delay in effecting this settlement, or to the notorious fact that obstinate resistance to claims, just in themselves, leads not to their suppression, but to advancement of others infinitely larger; a forced compliance with which would produce consequences never contemplated by the petitioners in the first instance.

We have, therefore, been of opinion, that the plan of Reform proposed by His Majesty's Ministers ought to be of such a scope and description as to satisfy all reasonable demands, and remove at once, and for ever, all rational grounds of complaint from the minds of the intelligent and the independent portion of the community.

By pursuing such a course, we conceive that the surest and most effectual check will be opposed to that restless spirit of innovation which, founding its open claims to public support on the impossibility and hopelessness of obtaining any redress of acknowledged abuses, aims in secret at nothing less than the overthrow of all our institutions, and even of the Throne itself.

We propose in one instance to make this a measure of disfranchisement. In the case of Nomination Boroughs—that system is one so entirely at variance with the spirit of the Constitution, so indefensible in practice, and so justly odious to the whole empire, that we could not consider any measure of Reform as otherwise than trifling and nugatory which did not include the abolition or purification of these boroughs.

We propose, therefore, to disfranchise all boroughs the population of which amounts to less than 2,000 inhabitants. This will effect the extinction of the worst class; and we propose also to deprive of one member all those whose population amounts to less than 4,000.

The purification of this latter class of boroughs, as well as of those cities and boroughs where the right of voting is enjoyed by close corporations, will, we think, be ensured by the extension of the Elective Franchise in them to all householders within the town or borough and parish entitled by the late Act to serve on juries, those who are rated to the relief of the poor, or to the inhabited house tax, at £20 per annum.

We propose to grant Representatives to all large and populous

towns of more than 10,000 inhabitants, of which there are unrepresented now in England about thirty.

The right of voting to be vested (as in the case of the purified
boroughs) in householders of £20 per annum.

In adopting this rate, we have considered that we have granted the
Elective Franchise to a constituent body including all the intelligence
and respectability of the independent classes of society. If we had not
felt ourselves called upon rather to extend than limit the Elective Franchise, we might perhaps have recommended the propriety of rendering it uniform by immediately merging in it all the multifarious and
inconvenient rights of voting now in existence.

We have, however, provided for their eventual extinction, and, in
the meantime, we trust, by the addition of an independent constituency,
and other arrangements, we shall effectually prevent the recurrence
of those scenes of corruption and political profligacy which too often
occur where the right of voting is vested in those whose want of
education and state of dependence render them quite unfitted for its
exercise.

We propose to give additional members to counties whose population amounts to more than 150,000, dividing them into districts,
leaving the forty shillings franchise as it now exists, but enfranchising
leaseholders of £50 per annum, and copyholders of £10 per annum.

Having adopted the principle of the amount of population as the
surest proof of the necessity of disfranchisement in some cases, and an
increase in the number of members in others, we could discover no
test more fixed and recognized than that of the last Parliamentary
census of 1821; upon which, therefore, our measure, both with regard
to counties and cities, is founded.

We next turned our attention to the necessity of diminishing the
expenses of elections, and we propose to accomplish this, by

The enforcement of residence;
The registration of votes;
The adoption of ballot;
The increase of the number of polling booths;
The shortening of the duration of the poll;
And in taking the poll (in counties) in hundreds or divisions.

We finally propose that the duration of Parliament should be limited
to five years.

We have embodied these arrangements and other measures of detail

connected with them in three Bills, the heads of which we annex to this
Report.

(Signed)   Durham.

James R. G. Graham.

John Russell.

Duncannon.

3   *The Introduction of the Bill*

(A) A DESCRIPTION FROM LORD BROUGHTON'S DIARY

At last came the great day—Tuesday, March 1. I went to the House
at Twelve o'clock, and found all the benches, high and low, on all
sides, patched with names. With much difficulty I got a vacant space
on the fourth bench, nearly behind the Speaker, almost amongst the
Opposition and the Anti-Reformers.

Lord John Russell began his speech at six o'clock. Never shall I
forget the astonishment of my neighbours as he developed his plan.
Indeed, all the House seemed perfectly astounded; and when he read
the long list of the boroughs to be either wholly or partially disfranchised there was a sort of wild ironical laughter, mixed with expressions of delight from the ex-Ministers, who seemed to think themselves
sure of recovering their places again immediately. Our own friends
were not so well pleased. Baring Wall, turning to me, said, "They are
mad! they are mad!" and others made use of similar exclamations,—
all but Sir Robert Peel; he looked serious and angry, as if he had dis-
covered that the Ministers, by the boldness of their measure, had
secured the support of the country. Lord John seemed rather to play
with the fears of his audience; and, after detailing some clauses which
seemed to complete the scheme, smiled and paused, and said, "More
yet." This "more," so well as I recollect, was Schedule B, which took
away one member from some boroughs that returned two previously.
When Lord John sat down, we of the Mountain cheered long and
loud; although there was hardly one of us that believed such a scheme
could, by any possibility, become the law of the land.

SOURCE. Lord Broughton, *Recollections of a Long Life*, ed. by Lady Dorchester (London:
John Murray Ltd., 1909–1911), Vol. II, pp. 86–88. Reprinted by permission of the
publisher.

Sir Robert Peel, with his usual quickness and sagacity, took care at the end of the debate to ask for an explanation of the £10 qualification for householders in towns, which certainly partook more of disfranchisement than any other reform, and was calculated to make the whole plan unpopular.

Burdett and I agreed there was very little chance of the measure being carried, and that a revolution would be the consequence. We thought our Westminster friends would oppose the £10 qualification clause; but we were wrong, for we found all our supporters delighted with the Bill.

(B) A DESCRIPTION FROM SIR JOHN LE MARCHANT'S DIARY

1 *March*—When Lord John had finished there was a dead silence which was broken by Sir John Sebrights's rising to support him. I went back to the Chancellor, who said "All will be well now. The only chance Peel had was to rise immediately after Lord John's speech and propose that the Bill should be read this day 6 months. He has allowed the opportunity to pass, and now will never recover it."

The astonishment—nay the shock produced by the sweeping provisions of the Bill, would I think have given Peel a large majority had he chosen to divide at this critical moment. I spoke to several staunch Reformers and found them wavering. They were like men taking breath immediately after an explosion. No one, however, was less himself than Peel. He sat pale and forlorn, utterly at a loss how to act. His countenance at times looked convulsed. The workings within him were evidently beyond his control. He was completely mastered, and yet he must have been in some degree prepared, for Lord Lowther had the day before learnt several particulars of Schedules A and B, though every precaution had been taken to ensure secrecy. [The Chancellor told me that the copies of the Bill had been made by Lord Durham's little girl. . . .]

SOURCE. Arthur Aspinall, ed., *Three Nineteenth Century Diaries* (London: Williams and Norgate, 1952), p. 13. Reprinted by permission of Ernest Benn Limited.

4   *The Commons Debate on the First Reform Bill*

(A) LORD JOHN RUSSELL, 1 MARCH 1831

Mr. Speaker: I rise, Sir, with feelings of deep anxiety and interest, to bring forward a question, which, unparalleled as it is in importance, is likewise unparalleled in difficulty, without my apprehension in the least degree being removed by the reflection that I have, on former occasions, brought this question before the consideration of the House; for if, on the other occasions, I have called the attention of the House of Commons to this subject, it has been upon my own responsibility—unaided by any one—involving no one in the failure of the attempt—though often completely gratified by partial success. But, Sir, the measure I have now to bring forward, is a measure, not of mine, but of the Government, in whose name I appear—the deliberate measure of a whole Cabinet, unanimous upon this subject, and resolved to place their measure before this House, in redemption of their pledge to their Sovereign, the Parliament, and to their country. . . .
It will not be necessary, on this occasion, that I should go over the arguments which have been so often urged in favour of Parliamentary Reform: but it is due to the question, that I should state shortly the chief points of the general argument on which the reformers rest their claim. Looking at the question, then, as a question of right, the ancient Statutes of Edward 1st contain the germ and vital principle of our political constitution. . . . [He proceeded to quote from two statutes of the reign of Edward. I.]

To revert again, for a moment, to ancient times; the consent of the commonalty of the land, thus declared necessary for the grant of any aid or tax, was collected from their Representatives consisting of two knights from each county, from each city two citizens, and from every borough two burgesses. For 250 years, the constant number of boroughs so sending their Representatives was about 120. Some thirty or forty others occasionally exercised or discontinued that practice or privilege, as they rose or fell in wealth and importance. How this construction of the House of Commons underwent various changes, till the principle on which it was founded was lost sight of, I will not now

SOURCE. *Hansard's Parliamentary Debates*, third series, Vol. 2, cols. 1061–1071, 1082–1083, 1086–1089.

detain the House by explaining. There can be no doubt, however, that at the beginning of the period I have alluded to, the House of Commons did represent the people of England. No man of common sense pretends that this Assembly now represents the commonalty or people of England. If it be a question of right, therefore, right is in favour of Reform.

Let us now look at the question as one of reason. Allow me to imagine, for a moment, a stranger from some distant country, who should arrive in England to examine our institutions. All the information he had collected would have told him that this country was singular for the degree which it had attained in wealth, in science, and in civilization. He would have learned, that in no country have the arts of life been carried further, no where the inventions of mechanical skill been rendered more conducive to the comfort and prosperity of mankind. He would have made himself acquainted with its fame in history, and above all, he would have been told, that the proudest boast of this celebrated country was its political freedom. If, in addition to this, he had heard that once in six years this country, so wise, so renowned, so free, chose its Representatives to sit in the great Council, where all the ministerial affairs were discussed and determined; he would not be a little curious to see the process by which so important and solemn an operation was effected. What then would be his surprise, if he were taken by his guide, whom he had asked to conduct him to one of the places of election, to a green mound and told, that this green mound sent two Members to Parliament—or, to be taken to a stone wall, with three niches in it, and told that these three niches sent two Members to Parliament—or, if he were shown a green park, with many signs of flourishing vegetable life, but none of human habitation, and told that this green park sent two Members to Parliament? But his surprise would increase to astonishment if he were carried into the North of England, where he would see large flourishing towns, full of trade and activity, containing vast magazines of wealth and manufactures, and were told that these places had no Representatives in the Assembly which was said to represent the people. Suppose him, after all, for I will not disguise any part of the case, suppose him to ask for a specimen of popular election, and to be carried, for that purpose, to Liverpool; his surprise would be turned into disgust at the gross venality and corruption which he would find to pervade the electors. After seeing all this, would he not wonder that a nation which had made such progress in every kind of knowledge, and which valued itself for its freedom, should permit so absurd

and defective a system of representation any longer to prevail? . . .
I end this argument, therefore, by saying, that if the question be one of
right, right is in favour of Reform—if it be a question of reason, reason
is in favour of Reform—if it be a question of policy and expediency,
policy and expediency speak loudly for Reform. I come now to the
most difficult part of this subject—the explanation of the measure,
which, representing the King's Ministers, I am about to propose to the
House. Those Ministers have thought, and, in my opinion, justly, that
it would not be sufficient to bring forward a measure which should
merely lop off some disgusting excrescences, or cure some notorious
defects; but would still leave the battle to be fought again with renewed
and strengthened discontent. They have thought that no half measures
would be sufficient—that no trifling, no paltering, with so great a
question could give stability to the Throne—authority to the Parliament—or satisfaction to the Country. Let us look, then, at what have
been the chief grievances in the representation, of which the people
have complained. . . .

  The chief grievances of which the people complain are these;—
First, the nomination of Members by individuals; Second, the Elections
by close Corporations; third, the Expense of Elections. With regard to
the first—the nomination by individuals—it may be exercised in one
of two ways; either over a place containing scarcely any inhabitants,
and with a very extensive right of election, or over a place of wide
extent and numerous population, but where the franchise is confined
to very few residents. Gatton is an example of the first, and Bath of the
second. At Gatton, the right is popular, but there is nobody to exercise
it: at Bath, the inhabitants are numerous, but very few of them have
any concern in the result of an election. We have addressed ourselves
to both these evils, because we have thought it essential to apply a
remedy to both; but they must, of course, be dealt with in different
ways. With regard to Boroughs where there are scarcely any inhabitants,
and where the elective franchise is such as to enable many individuals
to give their voices in the choice of Members for this House, it would
be evidently a mere farce to take away the right from the person exercising it, and to give it to the borough; and the only Reform that can be
justly recommended is, to deprive the borough of its franchise altogether.
I am perfectly aware, that in making this proposition we are proposing a bold and decisive measure. . . . The plan we propose is, therefore,
to meet the difficulty in front—as the Duke of Wellington and his
colleagues met it in the year 1829; and our measure will have the effect
of disfranchising a number of boroughs, as that measure disfranchised

a number of voters.[1] It would be a task of extreme difficulty to ascertain the exact proportion of the wealth, trade, extent, and population, of a given number of places, and we have, therefore, been governed by what is manifestly a public record—I mean the population returns of 1821, and we propose that every borough which in that year had less than 2,000 inhabitants, shall altogether lose the right of sending Members to Parliament. The effect will be, utterly to disfranchise sixty boroughs. But we do not stop here. As the hon. member for Boroughbridge (Sir C. Wetherell) would say, we go *plus ultra*. We find that there are forty-seven boroughs, of only 4,000 inhabitants, and these we shall deprive of the right of sending more than one Member to Parliament. We likewise intend that Weymouth, which at present sends four Members, shall, in future, only elect two. The abolition of sixty boroughs will occasion 119 vacancies, to which are to be added forty-seven for the boroughs allowed to send only one Member, and two of which Weymouth will be deprived, making in the whole 168 vacancies. Such is the extent to which Ministers propose to go in the way of disfranchisement. But, as I have already said, we do not mean to allow that the remaining boroughs should be in the hands of select Corporations—that is to say, in the possession of a small number of persons, to the exclusion of the great body of the inhabitants, who have property and interest in the place represented. It has been a point of great difficulty to decide to whom the franchise should be extended. . . . [He proceeded to discuss a number of unsatisfactory possibilities which he rejected.]

We therefore propose that the right of voting shall be given to householders paying rates for, or occupying a house of, the yearly value of £10 and upwards. Whether he be the proprietor, or whether he only rent the house, the person rated will have the franchise upon certain conditions hereafter to be named. At the same time, it is not intended to deprive the present electors of their privilege to vote, provided they be resident. . . . I shall now proceed to the manner in which we propose to extend the franchise in counties. The Bill I wish to introduce will give all copyholders to the value of £10 a year, qualified under the right hon. Gentleman's bill to serve on Juries, and all leaseholders for not less than twenty-one years, whose leases have not been renewed within two years, a right to vote for the return of Knights of the Shire. [Sir R. Peel asked, across the Table, the amount of rent which was necessary?] The right will depend upon a lease for

---

[1] 200,000 Irish freeholders were disfranchised by the Catholic Emancipation Act.

twenty-one years, where the annual rent is not less than fifty pounds.[2] It will be recollected that, when speaking of the numbers disfranchised, I said, that 168 vacancies would be created. We are of opinion that it would not be wise or expedient to fill up the whole number of those vacancies.[3] . . . Having gone through the several alterations proposed in England and Wales, in Scotland and Ireland, I now come to the result.[4]

The number of Members now belonging to this house is	658
The number to be disfranchised	168 [143]
Number remaining	490 [515]
Additional Members for Scotland	5 [8]
Additional Members for Ireland	3 [5]
Additional Members for Wales	1 [5]
Additional Members for the metropolis	8 [10]
New Members for large towns in England	34 [54]
Additional Members for counties in England	55 [61]
Total additional Members	106 [143]
Members of the House not to be disfranchised	490 [515]
Total	596 [658]

Making a decrease of sixty-two Members in the total number of Representatives. I will now state the number of additional persons who, I suppose, will be entitled to votes for counties, towns, and boroughs under this Bill:

	Persons
The number in towns and boroughs in England already sending Members will be increased by	110,000
The electors of towns (in England) sending Members for the first time I estimate at	50,000
Electors in London, who will obtain the right of voting	95,000
Increase of electors in Scotland	60,000
In Ireland, perhaps	40,000
Increase in the counties of England probably	100,000

It is my opinion, therefore, that the whole measure will add to the constituency of the Commons House of Parliament, about half a

---

[2] In the act as finally passed in 1832 the county franchise was extended to £50 tenants at will (a class of farmers subservient to their landlords) by the famous Chandos clause.

[3] In the act as finally passed in 1832 the vacancies were reduced to 143 and these were all redistributed.

[4] Figures in brackets are those for the act as finally passed in 1832. See also Appendix 2.

million of persons, and these all connected with the property of the country, having a valuable stake amongst us, and deeply interested in our institutions. They are the persons on whom we can depend in any future struggle in which this nation may be engaged, and who will maintain and support Parliament and the Throne in carrying that struggle to a successful termination. I think that those measures will produce a farther benefit to the people, by the great incitement which it will occasion to industry and good conduct. . . . It may be said too, that one great and injurious effect of the measures I propose will be, to destroy the power and privileges of the aristocracy. This I deny. I utterly deny that this plan can have any such effect. Wherever the aristocracy reside, receiving large incomes, performing important duties, relieving the poor by charity, and evincing private worth and public virtue, it is not in human nature that they should not possess a great influence upon public opinion, and have an equal weight in electing persons to serve their country in Parliament. Though such persons may not have the direct nomination of members under this Bill, I contend that they will have as much influence as they ought to have. But if by aristocracy those persons are meant who do not live among the people, who know nothing of the people, and who care nothing for them—who seek honours without merit, places without duty, and pensions without service—for such an aristocracy I have no sympathy; and I think, the sooner its influence is carried away with the corruption on which it has thriven, the better for the country, in which it has repressed so long every wholesome and invigorating influence. Language has been held on this subject, which I hope will not be heard in future. A call has been made upon the aristocracy—all who are connected with it have been summoned to make a stand against the people. Some persons have even ventured to say, that they, by their numerical strength, could put down what they call sedition. But the question at issue does not respect the putting down of sedition. The real question is, whether, without some large measure of Reform, the business of the country can be carried on with the confidence and the support of the people? . . .

To establish the Constitution on a firm basis, you must show that you are determined not to be the representatives of a small class, or of a particular interest; but to form a body, who, representing the people, springing from the people, and sympathising with the people, can fairly call on the people to support the future burthens of the country, and to struggle with the future difficulties which it may have to encounter; confident that those who call upon them are ready to join them heart and hand: and are only looking, like themselves, to the glory and welfare of England. I conclude, Sir, by moving for leave to bring in a Bill for amending the state of the Representation in England and Wales.

(B) T. B. MACAULAY, 2 MARCH 1831[5]

...Their [the ministers'] principle is plain, rational, and consistent. It is this,—to admit the middle class to a large and direct share in the Representation, without any violent shock to the institutions of our country....I consider this, Sir, as a practical question. I rest my opinion on no general theory of government—I distrust all general theories of government. I will not positively say, that there is any form of polity which may not, under some conceivable circumstances, be the best possible. I believe that there are societies in which every man may safely be admitted to vote.... Universal Suffrage exists in the United States without producing any very frightful consequences; and I do not believe, that the people of those States, or of any part of the world, are in any good quality naturally superior to our own countrymen. But, unhappily, the lower orders in England, and in all old countries, are occasionally in a state of great distress. Some of the causes of this distress are, I fear, beyond the control of the Government. We know what effect distress produces, even on people more intelligent than the great body of the labouring classes can possibly be. We know that it makes even wise men irritable, unreasonable, and credulous—eager for immediate relief—heedless of remote consequences. There is no quackery in medicine, religion, or politics, which may not impose even on a powerful mind, when that mind has been disordered by pain or fear. It is therefore no reflection on the lower orders of Englishmen, who are not, and who cannot in the nature of things be highly educated, to say that distress produces on them its natural effects, those effects which it would produce on the Americans, or on any other people,— that it blunts their judgment, that it inflames their passions, that it makes them prone to believe those who flatter them, and to distrust those who would serve them. For the sake, therefore, of the whole

SOURCE. *Hansard's Parliamentary Debates*, third series, Vol. 2, cols. 1191–1197.

[5]An edited version of this speech will be found in the Everyman edition of *Macaulay's Speeches*, but there are no substantial changes.

society, for the sake of the labouring classes themselves, I hold it to be clearly expedient, that in a country like this, the right of suffrage should depend on a pecuniary qualification. Every argument, Sir, which would induce me to oppose Universal Suffrage, induces me to support the measure which is now before us. I oppose Universal Suffrage, because I think that it would produce a destructive revolution. I support this measure, because I am sure that it is our best security against a revolution. . . . I, Sir, do entertain great apprehension for the fate of my country. I do in my conscience believe, that unless this measure, or some similar measure, be speedily adopted, great and terrible calamities will befall us. Entertaining this opinion, I think myself bound to state it, not as a threat, but as a reason. I support this measure as a measure of Reform: but I support it still more as a measure of conservation. That we may exclude those whom it is necessary to exclude, we must admit those whom it may be safe to admit. At present we oppose the schemes of revolutionists with only one half, with only one quarter of our proper force. We say, and we say justly, that it is not by mere numbers, but by property and intelligence, that the nation ought to be governed. Yet, saying this, we exclude from all share in the government vast masses of property and intelligence,—vast numbers of those who are most interested in preserving tranquillity, and who know best how to preserve it. We do more. We drive over to the side of revolution those whom we shut out from power. Is this a time when the cause of law and order can spare one of its natural allies? My noble friend, the Paymaster of the Forces, happily described the effect which some parts of our representative system would produce on the mind of a foreigner, who had heard much of our freedom and greatness. If, Sir, I wished to make such a foreigner clearly understand what I consider as the great defects of our system, I would conduct him through that great city which lies to the north of Great Russell-street and Oxford-street,—a city superior in size and in population to the capitals of many mighty kindgoms; and probably superior in opulence, intelligence, and general respectability, to any city in the world. I would conduct him through that interminable succession of streets and squares, all consisting of well-built and well-furnished houses. I would make him observe the brilliancy of the shops, and the crowd of well-appointed equipages. I would lead him round that magnificent circle of palaces which surrounds the Regent's park. I would tell him, that the rental of this district was far greater than that of the whole kingdom of Scotland, at the time of the Union. And then I would tell him, that this was an un-represented district! It is needless to give any more instances. It is needless to speak of Manchester, Birmingham, Leeds, Sheffield, with no representation; or of Edinburgh and Glasgow with a mock re-presentation. . . . It is government by certain detached portions and fragments of property, selected from the rest, and preferred to the rest, on no rational principle whatever. To say that such a system is ancient is no defence. My hon. friend, the member for the University of Oxford (Sir R. Inglis) challenges us to show, that the Constitution was ever better than it is. Sir, we are legislators, not antiquaries. The question for us is, not whether the Constitution was better formerly, but whether we can make it better now. In fact, however, the system was not in ancient times by any means so absurd as it is in our age. One noble Lord (Lord Stormont) has to-night told us, that the town of Aldborough, which he represents, was not larger in the time of Edward 1st than it is at present. . . . Does he remember how much England has grown in population, while Aldborough has been standing still? Does he consider, that in the time of Edward 1st this part of the island did not contain two millions of inhabitants? It now contains nearly fourteen millions. A hamlet of the present day would have been a place of some importance in the time of our early Parliaments. Aldborough may be absolutely as considerable a place as ever. But compared with the kingdom, it is much less considerable, by the noble Lord's own showing, than when it first elected burgesses. . . . We talk of the wisdom of our ancestors—and in one respect at least they were wiser than we. They legislated for their own times. They looked at the England which was before them. They did not think it necessary to give twice as many Members to York as they gave to London, because York had been the capital of Britain in the time of Constantius Chlorus; and they would have been amazed indeed if they had foreseen, that a city of more than a hundred thousand inhabitants would be left without Representatives in the nineteenth century, merely because it stood on ground which, in the thirteenth century, had been occupied by a few huts. They formed a representative system, which was not indeed without defects and irregularities, but which was well adapted to the state of England in their time. But a great revolution took place. The character of the old corporations changed. New forms of property came into existence. New portions of society rose into importance. There were in our rural districts rich cultivators, who were not freeholders. There were in our capital rich traders, who were not liverymen. Towns shrank into villages. Villages swelled into cities larger than the London of the Plantagenets. Unhappily, while the natural growth of society went on, the artificial polity continued unchanged. The ancient form of the representation remained; and precisely because the form remained, the spirit departed. Then came that pressure almost to bursting—the new wine in the old bottles— the new people under the old institutions. It is now time for us to pay a decent, a rational, a manly reverence to our ancestors—not by superstitiously adhering to what they, under other circumstances, did, but by doing what they, in our circumstances, would have done. All history is full of revolutions, produced by causes similar to those which are now operating in England. A portion of the community which had been of no account, expands and becomes strong. It demands a place in the system, suited, not to its former weakness, but to its present power. If this is granted, all is well. If this is refused, then comes the struggle between the young energy of one class, and the ancient privileges of another. Such was the struggle between the Plebeians and the Patricians of Rome. Such was the struggle of the Italian allies for admission to the full rights of Roman citizens. Such was the struggle of our North American colonies against the mother country. Such was the struggle which the *Tiers Etat* of France main- tained against the aristocracy of birth. Such was the struggle which the Catholics of Ireland maintained against the aristocracy of creed. Such is the struggle which the free people of colour in Jamaica are now maintaining against the aristocracy of skin. Such, finally, is the struggle which the middle classes in England are maintaining against an aristocracy of mere locality—against an aristocracy, the principle of which is to invest 100 drunken pot-wallopers in one place, or the owner of a ruined hovel in another, with powers which are withheld from cities renowned to the furthest ends of the earth, for the marvels of their wealth and of their industry. . . .

(C) SIR ROBERT PEEL, 3 MARCH 1831

. . . Sir, another and a still more alarming menace has been thrown out by the advocates of the Bill. I am told by them that the alternative before me is the adoption of that Bill, or civil commotion. I am to

SOURCE. *Hansard's Parliamentary Debates*, third series, Vol. 2, cols. 1337–1339, 1342– 1350, 1353–1356.

be deterred from forming a deliberate judgment on a most important public question by the prophetic visions of massacre and confiscation. Such were the words used last night by the hon. member for Calne [Macaulay]. Let me ask the friends of the Bill why I am to allow myself to be scared by this intimation? . . . Why am I to yield to popular clamour and violence, when the noble Lord opposite has not yielded to them when they demanded the Repeal of the Union? We were told last night, that if we rejected this proposition, we, the individual Members who so rejected it, would be held responsible for the consequences. "We will shift from our own shoulders," say his Majesty's Ministers, even at this early period of the agitation they foresee, "the responsibility of having provoked it. We have proved our incapacity to govern, but we will shew you our capacity to destroy, and hold you responsible if you obstruct us." Oh no, Sir! On their heads shall be the responsibility of this mad proceeding. I, for one, utterly disclaim it. For what am I responsible? Was it I who raised the stormy waves of the multitude? Was it I who manifested my patriotism by exerting all my powers to excite the people to discontent with the existing Constitution? . . . Did I, at a moment when the events of Paris and Brussels had caused great public excitement, when various causes were conspiring to agitate the public mind, did I express my misplaced admiration of the conduct of assembled thousands who were supposed to have flaunted in the face of their King the emblem of a foreign Revolution? Sir, if there be men who, having thus excited the passions of the people, and spurred their lazy indifference, bring forward the Question of Reform at a time when all prudential considerations, whether with reference to foreign or to domestic topics, ought to have forbidden such a step,—if, I say, disappointment should follow their rash undertaking, I will never, while I have a voice in this House, allow them to hold me or any other individual Member of the House responsible for the consequences of their infatuation. I am told that an appeal will be made to the people. I beg not to be included among those who are charged with making any one observation disparaging to the middle classes of society in this country. I repudiate such sentiment—sprung as I am, from those classes, and proud of my connexion with them. So far am I from underrating their intelligence or influence, that I tell you this,—you who talk of appealing to the people,—that unless these middle classes shall shew more prudence, more judgment, and more moderation than their rulers, I shall despair of the destinies of my country. There are happy indications, however, which induce me to think that the confidence which I repose in the prudence, the moderation, and the judgment of the middle classes of society has not been misplaced. . . . If I must appeal, not to the reason and calm judgment of this House, but to some extrinsic and higher authority,—the feelings and wishes of the people,—why, then, I have nothing to hope for but that, before the people of England approve of this Bill, they will listen to a calm and temperate appeal in behalf of what the noble Lord calls, with somewhat of cruel mockery, the old English Constitution. I hope they will consider that the Constitution of a Government is a matter of extreme delicacy and importance: that it is a most complex machine, not to be judged of by the examination of any isolated part which may be put forward for the purpose of exciting abhorrence; but demanding a comprehensive view, not only of the structure as a whole, but of its practical effects. . . . The Constitution of this country is not written down like that of some of our neighbours. I know not where to look for it, except in the division into King, Lords, and Commons, and in the composition of this House, which has long been the supreme body in the State. The composition of this House by representatives of counties, cities and boroughs, I take to be an intimate part of our Constitution. The House was so formed when they passed the Habeas Corpus Act—a law which, together with other wise laws, Mr. Cobbett himself desires to preserve, although, with strange inconsistency, whilst he cherishes the fruit, he would cut down the tree. This House was constituted on the same principle of counties, cities, and boroughs, when Montesquieu pronounced it to be the most perfect in the world. Old Sarum existed when Somers and the great men of the Revolution established our Government. Rutland sent as many Members as Yorkshire when Hampden lost his life in defence of the Constitution. Are we then to conclude that Montesquieu praised a corrupt oligarchy?—That Somers and the great men of that day expelled a king in order to set up a many-headed tyranny?—that Hampden sacrificed his life for the interests of a boroughmongering faction? No! the principles of the construction of this House are pure and worthy. If we should endeavour to change them altogether, we should commit the folly of the servant in the story of Aladdin, who was deceived by the cry of 'New lamps for old.' Our lamp is covered with dirt and rubbish, but it has a magical power. It has raised up a smiling land, not bestrode with over-grown palaces, but covered with thick-set dwellings, every one of which holds a free man, enjoying equal privileges and equal protection with the proudest subject in the land. It has called into life all

the busy creations of commercial prosperity. Nor, when men were
wanting to illustrate and defend their country, have such men
been deficient. When the fate of the nation depended upon the line of
policy she should adopt, there were orators of the highest degree placing in the strongest light the argument for peace and war. When
we were engaged in war, we had warriors ready to gain us laurels in
the field, or to wield our thunders on the sea. When, again, we
returned to peace, the questions of internal policy, of education of
the poor, and of criminal law, found men ready to devote the most
splendid abilities to the welfare of the most indigent class of the community! And then exclaims the noble Lord, with just and eloquent
indignation at the thought:—"And, Sir, shall we change an instrument which has produced effects so wonderful, for a burnished and
tinsel article of modern manufacture? No! small as the remaining
treasure of the Constitution is, I cannot consent to throw it into
the wheel for the chance of obtaining a prize in the lottery of Con-
stitutions." . . .

But if it be a question of right, and if the right be on the side of the
reformer, why, I would ask, does the noble Lord limit the franchise
to particular districts and particular classes? Why confine the privilege of voting to those who rent a House rated at £10 a-year. The
law knows no distinction in this respect between the contributors to
the support of the State. Yet the noble Lord not only refuses the
right of voting to persons rated at less than £10, but he also dis-
franchises many who contribute to the public taxes, and who now
possess the privilege of suffrage. I conceive the noble Lord's plan to be
founded altogether upon an erroneous principle. Its great defect, in
my opinion, is that to which an objection has been urged with great
force and ability by the hon. member for Callington. The objection is
this—that it severs all connexion between the lower classes of the
community and the direct representation in this House; I think it a
fatal objection, that every link between the representative and the
constituent body should be separated, so far as regards the lower
classes. It is an immense advantage that there is at present no class
of people, however humble, which is not entitled to a voice in the
election of representatives. I think this system would be defective if
it were extended further; but at the same time I consider it an in-
estimable advantage, that no class of the community should be able
to say they are not entitled, in some way or other, to a share in the
privilege of choosing the representatives of the people in this House.
Undoubtedly, if I had to choose between two modes of representation,

and two, only, and if it were put to me whether I would prefer that system which would send the hon. member for Windsor, or that which would return the hon. member for Preston, I should, undoubtedly, prefer that by which the hon. member for Windsor would be returned; but I am not in this dilemma, and am at perfect liberty to protest against a principle which excludes altogether the member for Preston. I think it an immense advantage that the class which includes the weavers of Coventry and the pot-wallopers of Preston has a share in the privileges of the present system. The individual right is limited, and properly limited, within narrow bounds; but the class is represented. It has its champion within your walls, the organ of its feeling, and the guardian of its interests. But what will be the effect of cutting off altogether the communication between this House and all that class of society which is above pauperism, and below the arbitrary and impassable line of £10 rental which you have selected? If you were establishing a perfectly new system of representation, and were unfettered by the recollections of the past, and by existing modes of society, would it be wise to exclude altogether the sympathies of this class? How much more unwise, when you find it possessed from time immemorial of the privilege!—to take the privilege away, and to subject a great, powerful, jealous, and intelligent, mass of your population to the injury—aye, and to the stigma, of entire uncompensated exclusion! . . . Now, Sir, I am content to try the merits of our present representative system by the hon. Member's [Macaulay's] own test. I repeat with him, that it is by tendencies, and not by accidents, that we are to judge of its merits. For the purpose of submitting those merits to that test, I wrote down this morning the names of those distinguished men who have appeared in this House, during the last forty or fifty years, as brilliant lights above the horizon, and whose memory, to quote the expression of Lord Plunkett, has had buoyancy enough to float down to posterity on the stream of time. I made this selection of these men, in the first instance, without a thought of the places they severally represented. I looked to their ability and their fame alone. If I have omitted any, their names may be added, but I believe the list I shall read will contain all the names that are of the highest eminence. It includes the names of Dunning, Lord North, Charles Townsend, Burke, Fox, Pitt, Lord Grenville, Sheridan, Windham, Perceval, Lord Wellesley, Lord Plunkett, Canning, Huskisson, Brougham, Horner, Romilly, Tierney, Sir William Grant, Lord Liverpool, Lord Castlereagh, Lord Grey. . . . These are the names of, I believe, the most distinguished men of the times in which they lived. They are twenty-two in number. Sixteen, on first entering public life, were returned for boroughs every one of which, without an exception, the noble Lord proposes to extinguish. Some few of these distinguished men owed, it is true, their first return to a more numerous body of constituents . . . but it is equally true that, for some cause or other, either the caprice of popular bodies, or the inconvenience of Ministers of the Crown sitting for populous places, in every one of these cases the honour of the populous place is relinquished for the repose of the small borough. . . . Now, then, I have applied your own test, I have looked not to accidents but to tendencies, and I ask you, whether the tendency of the present system of representation is not to secure to distinguished ability a seat in the public councils? But, after all, this question must be determined by a reference to still higher considerations. The noble Lord has pointed out the theoretical defects in our present system of representation; he has appealed to the people; he has desired them to accompany him to the green mounds of Old Sarum, and the ruined niches of Midhurst. I, too, make my appeal to that same people. I ask them, when they have finished poring over the imputed blots in their form of Government, when they have completed their inspection of the impurities of Old Sarum, and Gatton, and Midhurst, I ask them to elevate their vision, *Os homini sublime dedit*, to include within their view a wider range than that to which the noble Lord would limit them. . . . I lament—deeply lament, the time which has been chosen for the introduction of this measure. It is brought forward at a period of great excitement; when men are scarcely sober judges of the course which it is fitting to pursue. This has been always the case with Reform; it has been uniformly brought forward, either at the times of domestic calamity, or when the agitations of other States had infected us with extravagant and temporary enthusiasm for what was considered the cause of liberty. . . . We are arrived at 1831, and Reform is again proposed, whilst the events of the last year in Paris and Brussels are bewildering the judgment of many, and provoking a restless, unquiet disposition, unfit for the calm consideration of such a question. I, too, refer to the condition of France, and I hold up the late revolution in France, not as an example, but as a warning to this country. Granted that the resistance to authority was just; but look at the effects,—on the national prosperity, on industry, on individual happiness,—even of just resistance. Let us never be tempted to resign the well-tempered freedom which we enjoy, in the ridiculous pursuit of the wild liberty which France has established.

What avails that liberty which has neither justice nor wisdom for its companions—which neither brings peace nor prosperity in its train? It was the duty of the King's Government to abstain from agitating this question at such a period as the present—to abstain from the excitement throughout this land of that conflict—(God grant it may be only a moral conflict!)—which must arise between the possessors of existing privileges, and those to whom they are to be transferred. It was the duty of the Government to calm, not to stimulate, the fever of popular excitement. They have adopted a different course—they have sent through the land the firebrand of agitation, and no one can now recall it. Let us hope that there are limits to their powers of mischief. They have, like the giant enemy of the Philistines, lighted three hundred brands, and scattered through the country discord and dismay; but God forbid that they should, like him, have the power to concentrate in death all the energies that belong to life, and to signalize their own destruction by bowing to the earth the pillars of that sacred edifice, which contains within its walls, according even to their own admission, "the noblest society of freemen in the world."

5   *The Decision to Dissolve Parliament*

(A) MINUTE OF THE CABINET, 20 APRIL 1831

Your Majesty's confidential servants having taken into their most serious consideration the circumstances under which the Division of last night took place in the House of Commons,[1] and the effect of that Division, have arrived at the painful conclusion, that there is no reasonable hope of the ultimate success of the Reform Bill in the present House of Commons.

Earl Grey having communicated to them your Majesty's letter of yesterday's date, they have been impressed with the most lively gratitude for your Majesty's most gracious approbation of their humble services; and they must necessarily feel the deepest regret at finding themselves compelled to offer your Majesty advice which possibly may not meet with your Majesty's concurrence.

SOURCE. Henry Earl Grey, ed. *The Reform Act, 1832; Correspondence of the Late Earl Grey with William IV, 1830–1832* (London, 1867), Vol. I, pp. 225–226.

[1] On the Gascoyne amendment.

But, under the circumstances in which they are now placed, they can see no alternative consistent with the duty which they owe to your Majesty and to the country, but that of humbly recommending a dissolution of the present Parliament.

Your Majesty's confidential servants beg leave to add that they have not come to the determination of humbly offering this advice to your Majesty without having anxiously deliberated on the state of every part of the United Kingdom, and particularly of Ireland; and without having convinced themselves, from the best information they could collect, that the measure which they recommended would be perfectly consistent with the public safety.

(B) THE KING TO EARL GREY, 21 APRIL 1831

In the short letter which the King wrote to Earl Grey yesterday afternoon, in acknowledgment of the Minute of Cabinet submitted to him, His Majesty stated that the Minute involved matter of such deep importance to the interests of the country and to His Majesty's character, that he could not come to any decision upon it without mature consideration.

The question which has engaged his serious attention and his anxious reflection has been, whether he should subscribe to a proposal to which he has repeatedly stated objections which have not been removed, nor essentially weakened; or whether he should make up his mind to a second change of administration, within a very short space of time since his accession, at a period when so much of the welfare of this country, so much of the welfare of Europe, depend upon the stability of his Government, and upon the confidence which the adherence to a steady system of administration may inspire?

Such is the alternative upon which the King has had to decide; for, although it has not been presented to him in words in the Minute of Cabinet, His Majesty could not expect that his refusal to dissolve Parliament, when he had been so strongly urged to do so by his confidential servants, would not be followed by their resignation. . . .

The King does not disguise from Earl Grey and his confidential servants, that this apprehension of a frequent change of Government, so detrimental to the general interests of the country, has had a

SOURCE. Henry Earl Grey, ed., *The Reform Act, 1832; Correspondence of the Late Earl Grey with William IV, 1830–1832* (London, 1867), Vol. I, pp. 226–232.

principal share in producing his determination to yield to the proposed measure of a dissolution of Parliament; and that, upon this
occasion, he had considered very seriously whether the state of
parties and the feeling of the country offered a fair prospect of making any permanent arrangement which might relieve him from the
necessity of conceding that which is so repugnant to his feelings; and
that he is satisfied, from the best attention he has been able to give
to the subject, that he would not be justified in resorting to an
alternative which, in his opinion, would not have secured him for
many months against an event, the dread of which could alone have
induced him to contemplate an arrangement so much at variance
with the feelings he entertains towards his present Government,
nor indeed have secured him against the recurrence of the alternative. . . .

The King cannot close this letter without reminding Earl Grey,
that one of his objections to a dissolution was, that, in the present
temper of the people, those who should offer themselves for their
representatives might be called upon to pledge themselves to the
support of procedings greatly exceeding any measure of Reform
contemplated by his Government, or to which the King could have
been induced, *under the pressure of any circumstances*, to give his sanction;
and His Majesty having waived his general objections, expects that he
may rely with confidence upon his Government for the most stren-
uous and firm resistance and opposition to any attempt to introduce
and carry measures which would extend the principle of the present
Reform Bill, or which should have the effect of impairing the influence
and dignity of the Crown, and of curtailing the constitutional rights
of the monarchy.

His Majesty indeed considers that, if the result of a general election
should give to his Government a decided preponderance in the House
of Commons, advantage should be taken of it, not to re-establish the
Bill in its original shape, but to introduce such modifications as,
without producing any essential departure from the principle of the
measure, shall be calculated to conciliate the opponents of the Bill,
and to reconcile the *general* opinion and feeling of the country to it.
He considers the framers of the Bill to be pledged to those modifications of it which Earl Grey has stated to His Majesty, in detail, that
they were prepared to introduce, and that he was willing to admit.

6 The Defeat of the Second Bill in the House of Lords

(A) AN ACCOUNT BY CHARLES GREVILLE[1]

Newmarket, October 1st. On Monday the battle begins in the H. of L., and up to this time nobody knows how it will go, each party confident, but opinion generally in favor of the Bill's being thrown out. There is nothing more curious in this question that the fact that it is almost impossible to find anybody who is satisfied with the part he himself takes upon it, and that it is generally looked upon as a choice of evils, in which the only thing to do is to choose the least. The Reformers say, you had better pass this Bill, or you will have a worse. The moderate anti-Reformers would be glad to suffer the second reading to pass and alter it in Committee, but they do not dare do so, because the sulky, stupid, obstinate High Tories declare that they will throw the whole thing up, and not attempt to alter the Bill if it passes the second reading. Every man seems tossed about by opposite considerations and the necessity of accommodating his own conduct to the caprices, passions, and follies of others.

Riddlesworth, October 10th. At Newmarket all last week; all the Peers absent, here since Friday. Yesterday morning the newspapers (all in black)[2] announced the defeat of the Reform Bill by a majority of forty-one, at seven o'clock on Saturday morning, after five nights' debating. By all accounts the debate was a magnificent display, and incomparably superior to that in the H. of Commons, but the reports convey no idea of it. The great speakers on either side were:—Lords Grey, Lansdowne, Goderich, Plunket, the Chancellor, and Ld. Grey in reply, for the Bill; against it, Ld. Wharncliffe (who moved the amendment), Harrowby, Carnarvon, Dudley, Wynford, and Lynd-hurst. The Duke of Wellington's speech was exceedingly bad; he is in fact, and has proved it in repeated instances, unequal to argue a great constitutional question. He has neither the command of language, the power of reasoning, nor the knowledge requisite for such an effort. Lord Harrowby's speech was amazingly fine, and

SOURCE. L. Strachey and R. Fulford, eds., *The Greville Memoirs* (London: Macmillan & Co. Ltd., 1938), Vol. II, pp. 204–205. Reprinted by permission of the publisher.

[1] Charles Greville (1794–1865), Clerk of the Council, 1821–1859, kept a diary from 1817 to 1860, which was published posthumously.

[2] Not all of them—neither the Times nor Morning Herald.—G.

delivered with great effect; and the last night the Chancellor is said to have surpassed all his former exploits, Lyndhurst to have been nearly as good, and Lord Grey very great in reply. There was no excitement in London the following day, and nothing particular happened but the Chancellor being drawn from Downing Street to Berkeley Square in his carriage by a very poor mob. The majority was much greater than anybody expected, and it is to be hoped may be productive of good by showing the necessity of a compromise; for no Minister can make sixty Peers, which Ld. Grey must do to carry this Bill; it would be to create another House of Lords. . . .

(B) THE KING TO EARL GREY, 8 OCTOBER 1831

The King does not delay acknowledging the receipt of Earl Grey's letter, dated at half-past six this morning, reporting the Division which has taken place in the House of Lords upon the motion for the second reading of the Reform Bill.[3]

His Majesty would deceive Earl Grey if he were to say that the result is not such as he had long expected; . . . He considers it equally unnecessary to say, that the evil cannot be met by resorting to measures for obtaining a majority in the House of Lords which no Government could propose and no Sovereign consent to, without losing sight of what is due to the character of that House, to the honour of the Aristocracy of the country, and to the dignity of the Throne.

But His Majesty does not hesitate to say, that he would view as one of the greatest evils resulting from what has passed, the retirement from his Councils of Earl Grey and his colleagues, both as it would affect the interests of the country and those of Europe in general, at a period when so much is at stake, which a change of men and measures might interrupt and defeat. . . .

SOURCE. Henry Earl Grey, ed., *The Reform Act, 1832, Correspondence of the Late Earl Grey with Willaim IV, 1830–1832* (London, 1867), Vol. I, pp. 362–364.

[3] The Division had been,
Contents present, 128; Proxies, 30–158.
Not-contents, 150; Proxies, 40–199.
    Majority against the Bill, 41.

(C) MINUTE OF CABINET, 11 OCTOBER 1831

At a meeting of your Majesty's servants held to-day at the Foreign Office,

PRESENT:

The Lord Chancellor,	Viscount Melbourne,
The Lord President,	Viscount Palmerston,
The Duke of Richmond,	Viscount Goderich,
Earl Grey,	Viscount Althorp,
The Lord Holland,	Lord John Russell,
Sir James Graham,	Mr. Stanley,
	Mr. Grant,

the following Minute was unanimously agreed upon:

Earl Grey having communicated to your Majesty's servants the substance of what passed at the interview with which your Majesty was pleased to honour him yesterday at Windsor Castle, they beg leave humbly to express their unanimous feeling of gratitude and devotion to your Majesty for your Majesty's condescending expression of your continued confidence in their humble endeavours to promote your Majesty's service.

These endeavours will always be directed, as they have hitherto been, to the preservation of the honour of your Majesty's crown, and of the peace of your Majesty's dominions; and to secure these important objects, they cannot hesitate to express their entire concurrence in the opinion already submitted to your Majesty by Earl Grey, that it is absolutely indispensable that they should have the power of proposing to Parliament, at the commencement of the next Session, with the fullest indications of your Majesty's approbation and support, a measure of Parliamentary Reform founded on the same principles as that which has lately been rejected by the House of Lords, and of equal efficacy for the correction of those defects in the present state of the representation of the people in Parliament, which have become the subject of such general complaint.

Relying no less on their experience of your Majesty's uniform conduct towards them, than on the gracious assurances given by your Majesty to Earl Grey, they feel themselves bound, by every sentiment

SOURCE. Henry Earl Grey, ed., *The Reform Act, 1832, Correspondence of the Late Earl Grey with William IV, 1830–1832* (London, 1867), Vol. I, pp. 272–274.

of gratitude and duty, to devote themselves to the support of your Majesty's person and Government under all the difficulties of the present crisis.

7   *The Creation of Peers*

(A) MINUTE OF CABINET, 13 JANUARY 1832

. . . The general and intense anxiety which is felt for the success of that measure [parliamentary reform], the disappointment which attended the rejection by the House of Lords, in the last Session of Parliament, of the Bill which had been carried through the House of Commons by a great and decisive majority, and the revived hope of a more successful issue of the measure now before Parliament, have produced a feeling throughout the country which, adverting to the possibility of a second failure, cannot be contemplated without the greatest apprehension.

It might be hoped that an increased majority of the House of Commons, strengthened by the undiminished force of public opinion, would have its natural effect in disposing the House of Lords to acquiesce in a measure so supported.

It is however, with great pain, that your Majesty's servants find themselves compelled to acknowledge that they have not, up to the present moment, obtained any information which would encourage them to hope that there will not still remain in the House of Lords, a considerable majority against the Bill which is now in its progress through the House of Commons. . . .

It is with a view to a danger of this nature that the Constitution has given to the Crown the power of dissolving, or of making an addition to the House of Lords, by the exercise of the high prerogative of creating Peers, which has been vested in the King for this as well as for other important purposes.

By the first of these, if, in a difference between the two Houses, the House of Commons should not be supported by the Constituent Body, a return of representatives in unison with the public opinion may restore that harmony and agreement which are so essential to

SOURCE. Henry Earl Grey, ed., *The Reform Act, 1832, Correspondence of the Late Earl Grey with William IV, 1830–1832* (London, 1867), Vol. II, pp. 96–102.

the general security. The second can only be resorted to for the purpose of producing a change of conduct in the House of Lords, when the opinion of the people, strongly and generally expressed and identified with that of their representatives, leaves no other hope of terminating the existing division.

It is in such an extreme case alone that, in the opinion of your Majesty's servants, this exercise of your Majesty's prerogative of creating Peers for such a purpose could be justified. . . .

And here your Majesty's servants feel it to be their duty, in the first place, humbly to represent that it appears to them that the extent to which the Peerage, in such a case as has been contemplated, should be augmented, must be adequate to the necessity of securing the object in view. To make a new creation of Peers, which should prove ultimately ineffectual for its purpose would obviously be productive of the most unfortunate consequence. The acknowledged evil of adding to the Peerage, to carry a particular measure, would be incurred, and the danger, which it was intended to prevent, would not be avoided. . . .

In the present uncertain state of their information, they [the ministers] cannot take upon themselves to say, whether the addition of any given number of Peers would be sufficient, or whether it might not be more than the object in view would eventually demand. . . .

Upon these grounds your Majesty's servants beg leave humbly to submit to your Majesty the following conclusions:

First. That the expediency of making an addition to the Peerage upon the principles which have been stated, must depend upon your Majesty's being prepared to allow your servants the power of carrying it to the full extent which may be necessary to secure the success of the Bill, with which view it cannot be limited to any precise number at present.

Secondly. That if your Majesty shall be prepared for this consequence, the contemplated addition should be deferred till it may appear certain that, without such an addition, the strength of your Majesty's Government would be insufficient to bring to a successful issue the great measure, on which they believe the peace and safety of the country so essentially to depend. All which is humbly submitted by your Majesty's most dutiful subjects and servants.

(B) THE KING TO EARL GREY, 15 JANUARY 1832

The King received yesterday evening the Minute of a meeting of his confidential servants held on the 13th instant, transmitted to him by Earl Grey.

Important as is the subject, and serious as are the points submitted for his consideration and decision in this communication, they have too long engaged His Majesty's anxious attention, and presented themselves to his mind in every form in which they could be offered, to impose upon him the necessity of hesitating in the view which he is called upon to take of it, or of keeping Earl Grey and his colleagues in suspense as to the result of that view.

The Minute represents most ably and clearly the state and condition of public affairs, the situation of the country, and the general circumstances which, in the opinion of His Majesty's confidential servants, have reduced them to the painful necessity of submitting the advice which it conveys; and the King is not disposed to dispute the correctness of the reasoning, or the soundness of the argument, by which this advice is supported, always however with the reserve that it is applicable to the *existing* contingencies, and that the decision must be made upon due consideration of present circumstances, and of the necessity of incurring a serious evil in order to avert one which may prove yet more serious. . . .

To secure the Reform Bill against a second rejection in the House of Lords, and the country against the consequences apprehended from such result, the King is called upon to sanction an augmentation of the Peerage, to consent to an exercise of the prerogative for purposes and to an extent for which no precedent can be found of more recent date than the reign of Queen Anne. . . .

But when the King entered into this question, and showed the extent to which he might be considered prepared to concede, he did so upon the presumption (which, however, he admits not to have rested upon any assurance given to him), that the utmost number required would not exceed twenty-one, or at least not much exceed twenty-one; and that he was thus required to exercise his prerogative with a limitation, and not to an undefined extent; and it is impossible that he should not feel that there is a wide difference between that previous understanding and the case now submitted for his decision.

SOURCE. Henry Earl Grey, ed., *The Reform Act, 1832; Correspondence of the Late Earl Grey with William IV, 1830–1832* (London, 1867), Vol. II, pp. 108–114.

It is now stated, "that the expediency of making an addition to the Peerage must depend upon His Majesty's *being prepared to allow to his servants the power of carrying it to the full extent which may be necessary to secure the success of the Bill, with which view it cannot be limited to any precise number at present.*"

In other words, the King is required to surrender into the hands of his Ministers this important prerogative, to be exercised and applied without any other reserve or limit than that which their calculation or anticipation of the difficulties or opposition they may have to encounter shall produce: nor does the unrestricted surrender of this prerogative derive security from the character of those to whose honour and discretion His Majesty would not hesitate to confide it, inasmuch as the limits of its exercise must be dependent on circumstances, on contingencies of which the estimate may be precarious and uncertain, and which may therefore lead to an extension of the evil, far greater than His Majesty or his responsible advisers could ever have contemplated.

The King has stated freely his view of the question as now submitted to him, and has done so because he conceives that he owes it to himself and to his confidential servants not to shrink from the avowal of his sentiments; but, having done so, he will not, after having allowed that the resource should be effectual, and having, indeed, insisted upon the absurdity of incurring any risk by an insufficient addition to the House of Lords, if resorted to at all, deny to his Ministers the power "of acting at once up to the full exigency of the case;" it being understood that the contemplated addition shall be deferred till it may appear certain that, without such addition, the strength of the Government would be insufficient to bring the measure of Parliamentary Reform to a successful issue.

But His Majesty cannot give this pledge, nor consent to this surrender of the exercise of his prerogative, without attaching to it the positive and irrevocable condition, that the *creations of new Peers* shall, under no circumstances, exceed the three to which he has already agreed, namely, of Lord Francis Osborne, Mr. Dundas, and Sir John Leach; that the other additions shall be made by calling up eldest sons, or collateral heirs of Peerages where no direct heirs are likely to succeed, without reference to the objection which has been made, of throwing open the representation of counties or boroughs, which, if suffered to prevail, would have the effect of excluding many of those whom His Majesty considers the most eligible; that if these sources should prove insufficient (which, however, His Majesty can hardly conceive possible), recourse may be had to the Scotch and Irish Peerage for promotion to the English Peerage on this occasion, but that the selection shall be made from the oldest and most distinguished houses, so as not to detract from the value of the translation. . . .

His Majesty is satisfied, from an inspection of the lists, that, in subjecting his assent to the observance of a principle which he considers correct, and which he is therefore in duty bound to maintain, he does not require that which is unreasonable or impracticable, and therefore that he does not place his Government under embarrassment.

Even the throwing open the representations of counties and boroughs ought not to be objected to, when so much stress is laid upon the feeling throughout the country in favour of the present Reform Bill, and upon the general and intense anxiety which is felt for the success of the measure, as a fair opportunity will be thus afforded to the people of proving that His Majesty's Government have not been deceived in their estimate of that feeling. . . .

(C) SIR H. TAYLOR TO EARL GREY, 15 FEBRUARY 1832

My dear Lord, The King was not sorry to learn from the letter I had the pleasure of receiving from your Lordship this morning, that your interview with Lord Harrowby had been deferred until to-morrow, that he might have more time to ascertain the sentiments of some Peers with whom he had communicated. His Majesty attaches the greatest importance to what may pass at this interview, and looks to its result with intense anxiety. His hopes have been raised by your report of Mr. Wood's conversation with Lord Sandon, as well as by a note I received last night from Lord Wharncliffe, who mentioned that he was going to town to assist, and that a letter he had received from another friend gave him better hopes than anything he had seen.

Should these communications produce the desired effect, the King is satisfied that you and he will sincerely congratulate yourselves hereafter on having persisted in the endeavour to carry the measure by conciliatory means, rather than by resorting to a step to which he believes you to be as adverse as he is, on the honourable, constitutional, and high-minded principle which has influenced your con-

SOURCE. Henry Earl Grey, ed., *The Reform Act, 1832; Correspondence of the Late Earl Grey with William IV, 1830–1832* (London, 1867), Vol. II, pp. 223–225.

duct through life. His Majesty had, indeed, not scrupled to place himself in your hands, because he has felt confident that you were not disposed, as some others may be, to view this question (so objectionable in itself, so dangerous as a precedent) as one of expediency or of opinion, but as one of dire necessity, to which feeling must be sacrificed, when that painful sacrifice shall be imposed by a sense of duty arising out of the conviction, that an evil of greater magnitude could not be otherwise averted, and that it is more consistent with the interests of all classes of his Majesty's subjects, and therefore with the obligations of his station, that he should incur an evil and an inconvenience of which the extent is defined, than the risk and almost the certainty of a state of things of which the consequences could not be foreseen, nor the extent calculated.

The King is not ignorant to what degree your Lordship is urged and pressed by many who do not feel as you and he do on this point of adding to the Peerage, and who seem callous to the discredit which it may bring upon their body. He is not ignorant that they are endeavouring to drive you to the hasty adoption of a step which may not have become necessary, and to raise suspicions of the honesty and good faith of those who wish to come to some understanding, which shall prevent your making any attempt to secure by conciliation the result, and induce you to resort at once to a step which they treat with so much indifference. But His Majesty trusts you will not yield to this urgency, but that you will consult your own good feeling, and be guided by your own liberal sentiments in coming to a decision upon what shall be proposed to you.

In saying and in urging this, however, His Majesty desires he may be clearly understood; that he is far from wishing you to place the question in a situation which shall render its issue uncertain; and that he considers that if those who profess a disposition to support the second reading shall come to any understanding which shall offer ground for giving up the option which you have, to propose an addition to the House of Lords for the purpose of carrying the Bill, it must be clearly established that they are thereby pledged to carry the Bill subject to that understanding, and without introducing or supporting any alterations which shall be at variance with it. Unless you shall receive assurances which afford full security to this extent, His Majesty cannot expect you to commit yourself, or to risk uselessly the abandonment of an alternative which is at your option. The King has no objection to your stating to Lord Harrowby that such is his view of the rule on which you would be justified to proceed, if you think such communication calculated to forward the object of your interview.

His Majesty has learnt with extreme concern that the cholera is spreading, and is very sensible of the kind feeling which induces your Lordship to suggest that he should at once take up his residence at Windsor; but His Majesty is unwilling to alter his arrangements which, at any rate, had not been made with a view to a prolonged stay in London. He had intended, and still means, to go to St. James's for ten or twelve days, and afterwards to come from Windsor for court days and other occasions, as may be necessary and usual. He has no apprehension of the cholera, and does not think it right to excite alarm by appearing to run away from it.

8   *"The Days of May"*

(A) MINUTE OF CABINET 8, MAY 1832

Your Majesty's servants having been assembled to consider the situation in which they are placed by the vote of the Committee of the House of Lords last night, beg leave humbly to represent to your Majesty, that they find themselves deprived of all hope of being able to carry the Reform Bill through its further stages in a manner that would be for the advantage of your Majesty's Government, or satisfactory to the public.

So circumstanced, your Majesty's servants would naturally be led at once to tender to your Majesty, with every sentiment of respect and gratitude, the resignation of the offices which they hold from your Majesty's favour, if they did not feel it to be a paramount duty, not to withdraw themselves from your Majesty's service in a moment of so much difficulty, so long as they can contemplate the possibility of remaining in it with advantage to your Majesty and to the public interests, and without dishonour to themselves.

They, therefore, feel themselves bound humbly to suggest to your Majesty the expediency of advancing to the honour of the Peerage such a number of persons as might insure the success of the Bill in all its essential principles, and as might give to your Majesty's servants

SOURCE. Henry Earl Grey, ed., *The Reform Act, 1832; Correspondence of the Late Earl Grey with William IV, 1830–1832* (London, 1867), Vol. II, pp. 394–395.

the strength which is necessary for conducting with effect the business of the country.

In the opinion thus humbly submitted to your Majesty the Duke of Richmond alone of your Majesty's servants does not coincide. All which, &c.

(B) THE KING TO EARL GREY, 9 MAY 1832

It is not without the truest concern that the King acquaints his confidential servants that, after giving due consideration to the Minute of Cabinet which was brought to him yesterday afternoon by Earl Grey and the Lord Chancellor, and to the consequences of the alternative which it offers for his decision, of being deprived of the benefit of their further services, or of sanctioning the advancement to the Peerage of a sufficient number of persons to insure the success of the Reform Bill in all the principles which they consider essential, His Majesty has come to the painful resolution of accepting their resignations.

The King assures Earl Grey and his colleagues, that his sense of the value of their services, and of the zeal, ability, and integrity with which they have discharged their duties at a period and under circumstances of extreme difficulty, is unimpaired and undiminished; but His Majesty cannot reconcile it to what he considers to be his duty, and to be the principles which should govern him in the exercise of the prerogative which the constitution of this country has entrusted to him, to consent to so large an addition to the Peerage as that which has been mentioned to him by Earl Grey and the Chancellor to be necessary towards insuring the success of the Reform Bill in the House of Lords. . . .

(C) MINUTE OF CABINET, 18 MAY 1832

Your Majesty's servants having been assembled to consider the situation in which they now find themselves, in consequence of what

SOURCE. Henry Earl Grey, ed., *The Reform Act, 1832; Correspondence of the Late Earl Grey with William IV, 1830–1832* (London, 1867), Vol. II, pp. 395–396.

SOURCE. Henry Earl Grey, ed., *The Reform Act, 1832; Correspondence of the Late Earl Grey with William IV, 1830–1832* (London, 1867), Vol. II, pp. 432–434.

passed last night in the House of Lords, and having before them your Majesty's most gracious letter of this morning to Earl Grey, have agreed to submit to your Majesty as follows: They beg leave, in the first place, to renew to your Majesty the assurance of their grateful sense of your Majesty's most gracious wish that they should continue in your Majesty's councils; of their anxious desire to do everything in their power for your Majesty's ease and comfort; and, at the same time, of their deep regret that the event of last night's discussion in the House of Lords has not realised the hope which your Majesty entertained, and which they had cherished, that declarations expected to be made by the chief adversaries of the Reform Bill would have put an end to all fear of its not being carried, unimpaired in its principles and in its essential provisions, and as nearly as possible in its present form.

The first security, therefore, proposed in the Cabinet Minute of the 16th instant having failed, your Majesty's servants see no other possible except the second, which was submitted in the same Minute, viz. "such a creation of Peers as would afford your Majesty's servants sufficient power to overcome the opposition to the Bill." An assurance of your Majesty's consent to such a creation, in the event of any fresh obstacle arising, which should, in the humble judgment of your Majesty's servants, render it necessary for the success of the Bill, would afford to your Majesty's servants the security which, for the public safety, they feel themselves compelled to require as a condition of their continuance in office.

But they feel increased reluctance in pressing it upon your Majesty after the feelings expressed by your Majesty, in terms still stronger than on any former occasion, in your Majesty's most gracious letter of this morning to Earl Grey, terms which have given them more pain because they have formerly had your Majesty's gracious permission to recommend such a creation as might be sufficient to secure the success of the Bill, and your Majesty's specific consent to the number of forty-one Peers.

They beg most humbly to assure your Majesty that nothing could make them indifferent to your Majesty's honour, to your scruples of conscience, and to your future peace; still less could they overlook these considerations from any punctilious adherence to a mere form.

To insure them, on the contrary, there is no personal sacrifice which they would not readily make, provided it could be effectual for that purpose. But in the present state of the public mind, in the actual situation of the country, they are convinced that, whilst all the difficulties which with deep sorrow they now see pressing upon your Majesty would be greatly increased, they themselves would be deprived of all hope of acting usefully for your Majesty's service, either now or hereafter, if they were to continue in your Majesty's councils without a full and indisputable security, as was expressed in their former Minute and assented to by your Majesty, for insuring the speedy settlement of the Reform Bill in such a manner as would satisfy the just expectations of the public, and put an end to the agitation which now unhappily prevails.

All which, &c.

(D) THE KING TO EARL GREY, 18 MAY 1832

The King's mind has been too deeply engaged in the consideration on the circumstances in which this country is placed, and of his own position, to require that His Majesty should hesitate to say, in reply to the Minute of Cabinet left with him this afternoon by Earl Grey and the Lord Chancellor, that it continues to be, as stated in his recent communications to his confidential servants, His Majesty's wish and desire that they remain in his councils.

His Majesty is, therefore, prepared to afford to them the security they require for passing the Reform Bill unimpaired in its principles and in its essential provisions, and as nearly as possible in its present form; and with this view His Majesty authorises Earl Grey, if any obstacle should arise during the further progress of the Bill, to submit to him a creation of Peers to such extent as shall be necessary to enable him to carry the Bill, always bearing in mind that it has been and still is His Majesty's object to avoid any permanent increase to the Peerage, and therefore that this addition to the House of Peers, if unfortunately it should become necessary, shall comprehend as large a proportion of the eldest sons of Peers and collateral heirs of childless Peers as can possibly be brought forward. In short (to quote the Lord Chancellor's own words used in the interview between His Majesty, his Lordship, and Earl Grey), that the lists of eldest sons and collaterals who can be brought forward shall be completely exhausted before any list be resorted to which can entail a permanent addition to the Peerage.

SOURCE. Henry Earl Grey, ed., *The Reform Act, 1832; Correspondence of the Late Earl Grey with William IV, 1830–1832* (London, 1867), Vol. II, pp. 434–435.

Subject to these conditions, which have been already stated verbally, and admitted by Earl Grey and the Lord Chancellor, His Majesty assents to the proposal conveyed in the Minute of Cabinet of this day; and this main point being so disposed of, it is unnecessary that His Majesty should notice any other part of the Minute.

(E) FRANCIS PLACE'S ACCOUNT OF EVENTS, 11–18 MAY[1]

On Friday, May 11, a Birmingham deputation came to London, authorized to pledge the Birmingham Union to a rising. "Between eight and nine o'clock on the morning of the 11th I [Place] received a note from Mr. Parkes, saying that a spontaneous meeting of 100,000 persons had been held at Birmingham on the preceding afternoon at Newhall Hill; that expresses had been sent to all the London morning newspapers with an account of the proceedings, each of which would have a notice inserted. The people at Birmingham had determined not to pay taxes—to arm themselves. A deputation consisting of himself and others had arrived in London with a petition to the Commons, to be presented in the evening. They would be with me at ten o'clock. They intended being present at the Westminster meeting and at the Common Hall in the City of London, and to call upon the people of London to stand fast by them. All Birmingham had joined the Union. . . . At ten o'clock the Birmingham deputation and several other gentlemen, members of deputations from several important places, assembled in my library. We soon came to a clear understanding on the most material points. The state of the Government and the country was as freely as fully discussed. It was clear to us all that it would be impossible for the King to form any administration of which the Duke of Wellington was not placed at the head. It was as clear to us that the public was prepared to resist such an administration, and that if the means they employed should be unsuccessful in preventing its formation, they would at once openly revolt against it. The means of organising the people for effectual resistance were also discussed, and there was a general agreement that Birmingham was the place in which to hoist the standard of revolt, and it was understood that the first hostile

SOURCE. Graham Wallas, *Life of Francis Place* (London, 1898), pp. 299–301, 308–310, 314–321.

[1]The quotations are from the Place MSS in the British Museum.

defence against the Duke of Wellington's administration should be made there."

Next day (Saturday, 12th) a secret council of deputies was held. "It was agreed to consult during the day in every way with as many influential men as possible, . . . and to meet in a body with as many of the deputies from various parts of the country as could be collected together. Towards noon a meeting was held at a tavern in Covent Garden. Many deputies attended. The business was entered upon at once, and at once every one present was determined to go through with it. There was no reserve on any part of the whole of the case between the people and the Tories. The persons present were all men of substance; some were very rich men. All were persons of influence, and whom circumstances had made of considerable importance. Some were only known to others by name, some not in any way; but it seemed to be concluded that all who were present were good men and true, and there was as much confidence in each other's integrity as there could have been had each been the well-known friend of every one else. . . . It was clearly understood that in the event of Lord Wellington being appointed Premier and forming an administration, as every one expected would be at once attempted, that if necessary, as no doubt was entertained that it would be, open resistance should at once be made, and in the meantime all that could be done should be done to prevent such an administration being formed. . . . Were the proceedings reported to the Duke of Wellington and the King, they could use no means of personal annoyance. They could only proceed by using personal violence, and to this as yet they dared not resort. . . . Had they seized and imprisoned the persons of respectable men on a charge of a suspicion of high-treason, it would at once have caused an insurrection, a stoppage of trade and of the circulation of paper-money, and thus put an end to their power. . . . The reports which were probably made to the Duke of Wellington and Earl Grey must have increased their desire to have the matter settled."

. . . .

"It was now considered necessary that, as soon as it was ascertained that the Duke had formed an administration, all the deputies, excepting three sent by the three principal places, should return home and put the people in open opposition to the government of the Duke, while the leading reformers in London should themselves remain as quiet as circumstances would permit, and promote two material purposes: (1) keeping the people from openly meeting the troops in battle, supposing the soldiers were willing to fight them; (2) to take care to have such demonstrations made as would prevent the soldiers being sent from London, if it should turn out, as seemed next to impossible, that the mass of the people did not make these demonstrations themselves."

"It was very clearly seen that if a much more open and general run for gold upon the banks, the bankers, and the Bank of England could be produced, the embarrassment of the court and the Duke would be increased, and that if a general panic could be produced, the Duke would be at once defeated. . . . Among the persons present were two bankers, and although they were likely to be inconvenienced greatly, and perhaps to be considerable losers, they entered very heartily into the business. There was a general conviction that if the Duke succeeded in forming an administration, that circumstance alone would produce a general panic, and almost instantaneously close all the banks, put a stop to the circulation of Bank of England notes, and compel the Bank to close its doors; and thus at once produce a revolution. . . . While the discussion was going on, some one said, we ought to have a placard announcing the consequences of permitting the Duke to form an administration and attempting to govern the country, to call upon the people to take care of themselves by collecting all the hard money they could, and keeping it, by drawing it from Savings-Banks, from bankers, and from the Bank of England. This was caught at, and Mr. Parkes set himself to work to draw up a placard. Among the words he wrote where these,

"WE MUST STOP THE DUKE."

These words struck me as containing nearly the whole that was necessary to be said. I therefore took a large sheet of paper and wrote thus

TO STOP THE
DUKE,
GO FOR
GOLD.

"I held up the paper, and all at once said, 'That will do; no more words are necessary.' Money was put upon the table, and in less than four hours bill-stickers were at work posting the bills. The printer undertook to work all night, and to despatch at four o'clock on the next (Sunday) morning six bill-stickers, each attended by a trustworthy person to help him, and see that all the bills were stuck in every part of London. Other persons were engaged to distribute them in public-houses and in shops, wherever the people would engage to put them up, to send them to the environs of London by the carriers' carts, and thus cause as general as possible a display at once. Parcels were sent off by the evening coaches, and by the morning coaches of the next day, to a great many places in England and Scotland, and with some of these parcels a note was also sent, requesting the people to reprint them as posting-bills and as hand-bills." . . .

Next day, Friday (May 18), eleven days since the division in the Lords, and nine days since the acceptance of Grey's resignation, came the final crisis. . . ."Several persons," he [Place] says, "came to me before eight o'clock in the morning, each filled with apprehension, each having his own version of what had happened. All, however, had come to the same conclusion—resistance to the Duke at any cost, and in every possible way. Others came in, and at about half-past eight a gentleman came with a message from Sir John Hobhouse. He said there was to be a meeting[2] in Downing Street at noon, and Sir John wished me to write a letter to him, telling him all the facts I could, and giving him my opinion of the state of feeling among the people, as far as I could, and my view of prospective results. I therefore, as soon as I could dismiss the persons who were with me, and shut others out for a time, wrote as rapidly as I could the following letter: '*May 18, 1832. 9 A.M. Dear Sir John, The moment it was known that Earl Grey had been sent for, the *demand for gold ceased*. No more placards were posted, and all seemed to be going on well at once. Proof positive this of the cool courage and admirable discipline of the people. We cannot, however, go on thus *beyond to-day*. If doubt remain until to-morrow, alarm will commence again, and panic will follow. No effort to *stop the Duke by going for gold* was made beyond a mere demonstration, and you saw the consequences. What can be done in this way has now been clearly ascertained, and if new efforts must be made, they will not be made in vain.

"'Lists containing the names, addresses, &c., of all persons in every part of the country likely to be useful have been made, the name of every man who has at any public meeting shown himself friendly to reform has been registered. Addresses and proclamations to the people have been sketched, and printed copies will, if need be, be sent to every such person all over the kingdom. Means have been devised to placard towns and villages, to circulate hand-bills, and to assemble the people. So many men of known character, civil and *military*, have

[2]Of the Cabinet. . . .

entered heartily into the scheme, that their names when published will produce great effect in every desirable way. If the Duke come into power now, we shall be unable longer to "hold to the laws"; break them we must, be the consequences whatever they may; and we know that all must join with us to save their property, no matter what may be their private opinions. Towns will be barricaded, new municipal arrangements will be made by the inhabitants, and the first town which is barricaded shuts up all the banks. "Go for Gold," it is said, will produce dreadful evils. We know it will, but it will prevent other evils being added to them. It will *stop the Duke*. Let the Duke take office as Premier, and we shall have a commotion in the nature of a civil war, with money at our command. If we obtain the money, he cannot get it. If it be but once dispersed, he cannot collect it. If we have money we shall have the power to feed and lead the people, and in less than five days we shall have the soldiers with us. . . .' "

"I was confined to the house by the great number of persons who called upon me. They came from various parts of the metropolis, and were persons in various conditions of life. What each related respecting the anxious state of the public and their determination, was in unison, and might therefore be fairly considered the opinion of the people of London. . . . There were numerous meetings in many parts of London, and it was determined that in the event of the Duke's appointment being avowed in the Houses of Parliament, as it was expected it would be, that all the deputies and others who were up in London on the business of reform should go home by the speediest conveyances, call public meetings, appoint deputies to form a congress to meet at some proper place, to push the demand in every possible way, and to use every other means to embarrass and defeat the Duke.

"Birmingham was to take the lead, which it was prepared to do. The town was to be barricaded at once, and other towns were to follow the example. There was a very complete arrangement for procuring information of what was going on at Weedon Barracks, and there was a probability that the soldiers in these barracks would refuse to act against the people; and it was concluded that in such an event, few or none of the soldiers in other places would obey orders when it was seen that the people were able and willing to protect them. It was intended to seize as many of the families of the Tory Lords as possible, to carry them into the towns, and there to hold them as hostages for the conduct of the Duke towards the reformers. . . . No proceedings beyond those of causing a general demand for gold were to be taken in the first instance. It was to be kept as quiet as possible. It was quite certain that if the Bank closed its doors, and the supply of the markets ceased, a general tumult would immediately take place which no power the Government possessed could put down, nor could it continue in existence many days. Meetings would be called, and the necessary arrangements made to supply the metropolis with food. The army as well as every other department of military force would fall from the hands of the Government.

"An old Guardsman, a general officer, told me that he had seen his friend Lord Melbourne at the Home Office, and had told him the Duke could do nothing with the army, since he dared not move any part of it away from the metropolis, and that he could not use it with any effect in London; and that if he really understood the situation he would be placed in, he would never for a moment think of carrying on the Government by force."

"In this fearful state, this unparalleled situation, were the King and people placed; and the moment had arrived when the decision of one man, and he one of the silliest, was compelled to choose. . . . Truly were we in a lamentable situation when so much for good or evil depended on such a man as William the Fourth, King of England.

"The crisis was come; both Houses of Parliament were filled with members, and with as many strangers as could obtain admission. An immense concourse of people was assembled outside the Houses, and everybody waited the expected announcements with the utmost anxiety. It was fearfully apprehended that the Duke would be appointed; all confidence in the patriotism of the King had subsided, and the worst consequences were anticipated. The deputies from the towns in various parts of the kingdom had made preparations for their departure, and the evening papers had their forms standing ready to insert the announcements in the Houses of Parliament in second editions, to be forwarded by the mails and coaches to every part of the United Kingdom. In a state of indescribable apprehension and terror, Earl Grey in the Lords, and Lord Althorp in the Commons, announced the exhilarating fact that Ministers, having secured the means to pass the Reform Bills without mutilation, would continue in office.

"At half-past five o'clock, while sitting with some gentlemen waiting to receive the news that they might determine on the course it would be advisable to take, Mr. Howard, a gentleman who had gone to the House of Commons for the purpose of hearing the communication expected to be made, came in in breathless haste, and said he had just heard Lord Althorp make the declaration of his continuance in office, with full powers to carry the Bills. Mr. Howard was scarcely gone when, in a state of high enthusiasm, Sir John Hobhouse came and confirmed the information Mr. Howard had given us. 'An immense load had,' he said, been removed from the minds of all, and pleasant sensations would now take the place of the all but too well grounded apprehensions of most extensive evils, whatever good might ultimately be obtained, and that the people might honestly gratify themselves with their own manly, steady, courageous conduct, which had compelled the unwilling decision in their favour. Sir John stayed but a few minutes. Like every one else, he was eager to spread the good news as far and as wide as he was able.

"On the next morning I was informed that the King determined to appoint Earl Grey in consequence of the following circumstance: At about two o'clock a gentleman came to Earl Grey privately. He was commissioned by the Bank directors to inform him that if nothing was settled in time to be forwarded to the country by the mails, they apprehended that the depositors in Savings-Banks would generally give notice to withdraw their deposits, and convert the amount into cash. That this being known, other persons would also demand gold for paper, and that the run upon all the banks would, in a few days, compel them to close their doors. That Earl Grey requested this gentleman to proceed to the Duke of Wellington and make the communication to him. He did so, and the Duke having immediately made a similar communication to the King, Earl Grey was restored to office with the power he desired. This information was given me by a confidential person of a Cabinet Minister, with an injunction by him that I was not to use his name."

9   *The Significance of the Reform Act of*
1832—The Views of Three Historians

(A) ARTHUR ASPINALL

The consequences of the Act were by no means such as had been expected either by its supporters or its opponents. The Tory *Quarterly*

SOURCE. Arthur Aspinall, ed., *Three Early Nineteenth Century Diaries* (London: Williams and Norgate, 1952), Introduction, pp. xxx–xxxi. Reprinted by permission of Ernest Benn Limited.

Review declared that the character of the House of Commons would be degraded by the return of swarms of "intriguing and clever country attornies . . . hungry soldiers of fortune . . . bankrupts in trade and in character . . . street orators, itinerant lecturers and venal writers for the Press—a noisy and turbulent generation of glib talkers and shallow thinkers." But the personnel of the first Reformed Parliament proved to be remarkably like the old. It has been shown that there was no appreciable increase in the number of representatives of mercantile and industrial interests. The last unreformed House of Commons contained 33 bankers, 62 members representing East India interests, 34 representing West India interests, and 51 general trade (though some allowance has to be made for overlapping interests). Since the beginning of the eighteenth century, therefore, a silent revolution had been in progress, transforming the character of the House, whereby, even in the unreformed Parliament, commercial, manufacturing, banking, East India and West India interests had secured, not, indeed, adequate, yet substantial representation; and these powerful minority interests had materially contributed to a large change in the country's fiscal and commercial policy since 1820.

Wellington and his friends were wrong in thinking, not only that a reformed House of Commons would be "a democratical assembly of the worst description," but also that the Church-and-King party would cease to exist as an influential party, that the few Tories who might find their way into the House would never be capable of forming a Government, and would be driven, in self-defence, to unite with the Whigs against a great new Radical party. Within three years the party had sufficiently recovered its parliamentary strength to enable a Conservative Government to be formed, and the Tories had an immense majority in the Lords. And in 1837 the Radical party was shattered at the General Election.

The Tories were wrong, too, in believing that a revolution, though bloodless, would quickly follow the passing of the Bill. They did not see how the Irish Union, the Empire, the Church of England, the House of Lords, or even the Monarchy, could long survive. They were confident, and rightly so, that the Bill could never be a final measure—that it was merely the first instalment of a series of constitutional changes which would lead to a pure democracy. In the main, however, they were right in their diagnosis, though the process of change and disintegration took much longer than they expected. The power of the Crown has completely disappeared though the institution has survived; and the Crown has ceased to be an effective symbol of the unity of the Empire which the grant of self-government to the colonies ended by destroying. The Church of England has survived, like the House of Lords, but both institutions retain but a shadow of their former power and prestige. The redistribution of property has proceeded to such lengths that the Tories of 1832 might well have felt, could they have witnessed the changes of the last forty years, that their worst fears had been realised.

(B) CHARLES SEYMOUR

The immediate results of the redistribution of 1832 were naturally more striking than those proceeding from the application of the qualification clauses. The latter did not greatly affect the county electorate, and the alteration in the character of the borough constituency was largely gradual. So far as the effect on nomination was concerned, the opening of the close boroughs was not so complete as the absolute disfranchisement, which killed the system altogether in the boroughs of Schedule A that no longer had any representation. In the redistribution, moreover, are to be noted such democratic tendencies as manifested themselves in the Reform Act. The disfranchisement of the working classes which resulted from the qualification clauses, made that part of the legislation a purely middle class measure. But the redistribution, by its attack on the proprietors of boroughs, and by its enfranchisement of the industrial towns and their large population, took a decided step in the democratic direction.

So far as regards the balance of parties the Liberals would have gained even without redistribution. The opening up of the close boroughs far more than offset the advantage won by the Conservatives through the new county qualifications. But the great gain of the Liberals was through the redistribution of seats. The disfranchisement of the rotten boroughs eliminated the most powerful of Tory factors, and the newly enfranchised towns became the mainstay of Liberal strength during the generation that succeeded the passing of the Reform Act. But while the conditions which had guaranteed Tory supremacy were thus altered, Tory power was by no means annihilated. Notwithstanding the destruction of Tory nomination boroughs and

SOURCE. Charles Seymour, *Electoral Reform in England and Wales, 1832–1885* (New Haven: Yale University Press, 1915), pp. 101–103. Reprinted by permission of the publisher.

the formation of many constituencies destined for Liberal control, the Conservatives, strong in the counties, were able in many of the boroughs of moderate size to wage the contest on almost equal terms.

The immediate political effects of the Reform Act thus proved less striking than many had anticipated. Both the king and the ministers overrated the changes that would take place, and attached too little importance to the strength of the old influences by which the House of Commons was formerly returned. The ministers believed that the power of the Tories was annihilated through the destruction of their nomination boroughs, and considered that the Radicals and the rising tide of democracy were the chief dangers of the future. Inspired by this apprehension, the Whig ministers left many bulwarks of aristocratic control by which the Conservatives were destined to profit.

But in their fear of the Radical danger which might rise from the new enfranchisement, the Whigs made a miscalculation. As Roebuck said, the battle of the thirty years that followed the Reform Act was destined to be not between the Whigs, representing aristocracy and wealth on the one hand, and violent democracy on the other; but rather between the two types of wealth and property: the landed proprietors and the manufacturing capitalists. In either case wealth and property remained in control. The old influences by which the House of Commons had been elected still retained much of their importance, and while the system of nomination was broken, it was by no means destroyed. Moreover the control of the two aristocratic parties was maintained in nearly all of the older constituencies and some of the new, in part by the manipulation of the registration system, in part by the exercise of corrupt influence. . . .

(C) NORMAN GASH

. . . The first Reform Act was both a landmark and a turning-point, but it would be wrong to assume that the political scene in the succeeding generation differed essentially from that of the preceding one. . . .

In fact the pre-1832 period contained many new features which it transmitted to the future; and the post-1832 period contained many old features which it inherited from the past. Between the two there is indeed a strong organic resemblance. This is not to say that the

SOURCE. Norman Gash, *Politics in the Age of Peel: A study in the Technique of Parliamentary Representation, 1830–1850* (London: Longmans Green & Co. Ltd., 1953), pp. x–xi, 3–5, 8–12, 23–24, 28–29. Reprinted by permission of the publisher.

Reform Act achieved nothing. Its ultimate effects were considerable and there were some interesting, and rather unexpected, immediate effects. But the continuity of political fibre was tough enough to withstand the not very murderous instrument of 2 Wm. IV., c. 45. As will be seen in subsequent chapters there was scarcely a feature of the old unreformed system that could not be found still in existence after 1832. Thus many small pocket boroughs had been abolished by the Reform Act but over forty in England and Wales alone, together with a dozen more that regularly returned members of particular families, survived into the third quarter of the nineteenth century. Corrupt constituencies, open to the highest bidder, occupied a place in the reformed structure of representation and two of them, Sudbury in 1844 and St Albans in 1852, were disfranchised for gross and systematic venality. The ancient profession of borough-monger still survived here and there in congenial spots; and almost everywhere the tribe of solicitors and agents who grew fat on contested elections were promoting these operations for their financial rather than their political significance. There was no legal limit to the amount of money that could be spent on parliamentary elections and fortunes could be dissipated on a political career almost as easily as in the reign of George III. Great peers still sent their nominees to the lower house. Landowners, merchants, clergy of all denominations, shopkeepers, employers, publicans, customers, and clients, habitually exercised their social and economic influence for political purposes. Even the enfranchisement in 1832 of new industrial towns sometimes meant no more than the addition of landlords, such as the Ramsden family at Huddersfield, or industrialists, such as John Guest at Merthyr, to the existing "electoral influences" listed by any competent parliamentary guide. Nearly every constituency had some form of corruption peculiar to itself; and the borough electors as a class, whether old franchise holders or new £10 householders, customarily accepted, and often demanded, bribes. As a last resort, physical force, sometimes of an extreme and unpleasant nature, was used to produce the required verdict on the hustings. Gang warfare between the hired bullies of rival political magnets, and electoral intimidation by radical mobs, were spectacles to which early Victorian England was hardened if not reconciled.

.   .   .   .   .

The parliamentary debate on the reform bill began in March 1831 and continued intermittently until the summer of 1832. Looking back now on that involved and protracted discussion, on the three successive English bills, the two Irish and the two Scottish bills, on the vehement argument in parliament, and the even more vehement participation of the public in that argument, it is clear that given the contemporary political assumptions accepted by both sides the tories were in the right. Almost every point that they made, every fear that they expressed, were good points and well founded fears, even though the whig majority rejected their validity and denied their justification. Sooner or later all the major prophecies of the opposition came true. In some cases it took a century where they had anticipated a few decades; in others their predictions were vindicated within fifteen years where they themselves could scarcely have foreseen so sudden an onset of disaster. But taken as a whole the tory case against the reform bill was an accurate analysis of the real consequences of reform. That in itself, had it been accepted by their opponents, might have been sufficient to destroy the bill; since these consequences were so obnoxious, even in anticipation, to the majority of both parties in parliament, that it was imperative for the whigs to deny the accuracy of the opposition forecasts if they wished to retain the support of their own followers. For except on the specific measure before them there was a substantial amount of agreement between the parliamentary reformers and anti-reformers on political fundamentals; and conversely, therefore, agreement on what were political undesirabilities. Neither party was democratic; indeed, that adjective was still a term of abuse or condemnation among the ruling classes, and whigs as well as tories carefully dissociated themselves from its implications. Neither party was royalist in the sense of being a party pledged to the person of the monarch. Both were monarchical, in the sense of being a party anxious for the maintenance of the crown as an integral part of the constitution. Both were oligarchic and aristocratic; and though sensitive to public opinion both were opposed to demagogy. They were therefore in the position of two physicians, working according to the same science, but differing in their interpretation of a particular case. If the whigs had accepted the tory prognosis, they could scarcely have prescribed the remedy they did. Nevertheless, the tory prognosis was the correct one.

The case of the opposition was clear enough. Whether expressed confusedly by Wetherell, intemperately by Croker, or moderately by Peel, the common attitude can easily be distinguished among the intricate and laborious details of minor argument over schedule and franchise. In the first place the bill would inevitably destroy the

existing balance of the constitution. Already the influence of the crown
based on the control of patronage had been so diminished during
the two preceding generations that it now scarcely counted in the
scales. Under the new system the last major prerogative of the crown—
the choice of ministers—would be confined within such narrow limits
that in effect ministers would henceforth be imposed on the crown
by the popular assembly. . . .

What was true of the position of the Crown applied also to the
House of Lords. The strengthening of the popular part of the legislature meant a corresponding decline in the influence of the non-elective
house. Every diminution of aristocratic influence in the representative
system would widen the difference between the two houses of parliament and deprive the constitution of the checks and balances implicit
in the character of the House of Lords. So much emphasis was laid
by the reform bill on the popular aspect of the legislature that even
while the fate of the measure was still undetermined, the power of
the House of Lords seemed to be visibly shrinking.

.   .   .   .

No doubt fear sharpened the imagination, and a natural desire to
score in a debate exaggerated the pessimism of the tory opposition.
But it is clear that the debate over the reform bill of 1831 went to the
roots of political philosophy; and that when stripped of ephemeral
argument and selfish motive there remained at the core of the tory
position a genuine body of principles ranged against the whole spirit
of the Reform Act. Certainly the succeeding century was to vindicate
in an impressive fashion the correctness of their prophecies. On this
high historic and philosophical plane, therefore, the tory case against
reform was irrefutable.

Politics, however, are rarely fought out in such a rarefied atmosphere. A party enjoying the freedom of opposition may be able to
indulge in speculative refinements and look to the ultimate consequences of governmental actions. Politicians in office work within
a much narrower and more practical context. If the tories were the
better historians, philosophers, and prophets, the whigs were the
better politicians. What counted for them was not the verdict of
posterity but the force of contemporary society. The whigs could not
afford, and perhaps had no right, to look too far ahead. "Distant and
eventual," had pronounced the greatest of all whigs, Sir Robert
Walpole, "must yield to present dangers." Moreover in the long run
the politician is the servant of the forces he directs. The deliberations

of the cabinet committee on reform, and the Reform Act itself, were only symptoms of a much wider movement in the country. To ascribe solely to the decisions of a handful of ministers or to a single statute the immense political developments after 1832 is scarcely a tenable proposition. The whigs must bear responsibility for the Reform Act of 1832, but as instruments rather than as creators. The whole flank of the powerful intellectual position of the tories could be turned by one short question. What alternative was there to the whig proposals?

. . . .

The question narrowed itself therefore not to the principle but the degree of reform. Here the whig scheme, arbitrary and illogical as it was, represented with rough accuracy the most that could be pushed through parliament and the least that would satisfy the country at large. That the tories regarded it as revolutionary and the more extreme radicals as a betrayal was a reasonable indication of its value as a national solution. But that sooner or later something in the way of parliamentary reform must take place was apparent to most. With all its merits, the unreformed system had by 1830 one gross demerit. It was not regarded as satisfactory by the bulk of informed and influential opinion in the country. It was this practical consideration that was the strength of the whig case. It was never better expressed than by Melbourne in the House of Lords on the occasion of the second reading of the reform bill in 1831. He acknowledged frankly that he had previously resisted reform.

"But [he added] all experience proves, when the wishes of the people are founded on reason and justice and when they are consistent with the fundamental principles of the constitution, that there must come a time when both the legislative and executive powers must yield to the popular voice or be annihilated. . . ."

Indeed, reading this speech, suffused as it is with a kind of melancholy eloquence, one is reminded of the calm considered presentation of the case against reform put forward by Peel. Despite differences of background and temperament, Peel and Melbourne were together perhaps the truest diagnosticians of the reform crisis; the one opposing without hope, the other assisting without desire.

The defence of the whigs therefore is that they offered a practical remedy for a felt grievance. What the tories said was true; but what the whigs did was necessary. They satisfied in a rough but substantial fashion the immediate demand in the country for parliamentary reform.

. . . .

When the House of Commons went into committee on the first reform bill, Lord John Russell explained that on the question of enfranchisement the ministers did not look solely to population; they also took into account commercial capital and enterprise. Hence the population test was not a rigid rule. Indeed the ministers proposed "as a counterbalance to the pure principle of population, to give representation to large towns possessed of manufacturing capital and skill". A few months later, when introducing the second reform bill in June 1831, Russell elaborated this simple proposition by arguing that under the new scheme the members for England and Wales would be composed of about 150 county and 280 borough representatives. The borough members fell into two categories: those representing great cities and towns, including all the big manufacturing interests, such as wool, cotton, coal, and the potteries; and the remainder who numbered about a hundred, drawn from boroughs with a population of from three to six thousand, not immediately representing any interest, but perhaps in consequence "better qualified to speak and inform the House on great questions of general interest to the community". Even if this latter class did not represent the commercial interests, it is clear that they were designed to represent interests of a social or political type. At a later stage in committee Russell said that it was imperative to give representation to the populous industrial areas of the north but that the ministry had deliberately retained a class of small boroughs in order to ensure the representation of certain elements in the population that would otherwise be unrepresented. Here he was specifically referring to the forty boroughs of Schedule B (deprived of one member) and the additional thirty boroughs left intact although they did not possess a large constituency. The argument, however, is still relevant. It was a fundamental point of the bill not to produce uniformity but to ensure that a mass of interests great and small, industrial and social, were adequately represented in the House of Commons. The great argument against the unreformed system was not its anomalous structure but the fact that it left unrepresented or insufficiently represented certain important interests and gave representation on a lavish scale not to interests but to individuals.

. .

The whigs were in effect asking the tories not to surrender the powers of the aristocracy but to preserve those powers by opening their ranks and enlarging their basis. They denied that an aristocracy that was truly such—resident, public-spirited, of high private character and carrying out a national service—could lose its legitimate influence. But the constitution could not last much longer without "an additional infusion of popular spirit, commensurate with the progress of knowledge and the increased intelligence of the age". It followed from this attitude that what the whigs expected to produce by the Reform Act was what in fact largely resulted. The strength and homogeneity of the aristocratic ruling classes, as witnessed in parliament, in the government, and in local administration, remained substantially intact after 1832; though to a greater extent than ever before public opinion, after its signal demonstration during the reform crisis, exercised ultimate control over the extent and direction of that rule. Ostensibly power lay in the same hands as before; but henceforth no politician on either side of the House could ignore with impunity the new responsibility which rested upon their chamber. He did not think, observed Hobhouse shrewdly in March 1831, that by the reform bill, or any other plan of reform, "the complexion of the House, as to the members returned to it, would be much changed. The motives however that sent men into it would be totally different."

PART II
The Second Reform Act of 1867

INTRODUCTION

The Whigs had argued that because the First Reform Act was so extensive, it would be a final settlement; while the Tories had claimed that on the contrary it would inevitably lead to further changes. The latter were right in the long run, but in fact the Reform Act remained in effect for a generation, which is virtually an eternity in politics. It is true that both Prime Ministers who presided over the constitutional revolution of 1866–1867 were young members of the great Reform Ministry of the 1830s, but the passing of the Second Reform Act was in both cases the last important event of their political lives. Its passage was really the work of the generation of Gladstone and Disraeli and their juniors.

The Radicals and especially the politically minded working classes outside Parliament were soon disillusioned by the results of the Reform Act of 1832. The demand for a really democratic reform of Parliament was made most dramatically by the great Chartist movements of 1838–1839, 1842, and 1848, but these had little direct effect on parliamentary opinion. The Radicals in the House of Commons, however, continued to urge further extension of the franchise and vote by ballot. In 1851 they carried a reform motion introduced by Locke King, despite the opposition of the Liberal Ministry of Lord John Russell, now Prime Minister. With this defeat Russell promised, himself, to bring in a new reform bill.

He had one prepared for the session of 1852 but was defeated on another issue and driven out of office before any action could be taken on it. A year later he joined the Coalition Ministry of Lord Aberdeen on the understanding that he would bring in another reform bill, which he did in 1854, but he was forced to abandon it because of the Crimean War. In 1859 the minority Conservative Government sought to settle the matter with a very limited bill, which was defeated by the Liberal majority because it did not go far enough. The following year Russell brought in a more generous measure that would have extended the vote to householders paying £6 rent a year and redistributed 25 seats. This failed because of the apathy of the House of Commons at that time and the issue remained dormant as long as the antireform Lord Palmerston remained the Liberal Prime Minister. On Palmerston's death in 1865, Russell, now in the House of Lords, once again became Prime Minister and determined to settle the reform issue before his final retirement.

The England of the 1860s was very different from that of the 1830s. Industry had continued to expand and diversify, while London and the great provincial cities had continued to grow apace. An efficient network of railways now bound the country tightly together as never before, and the stagecoach had become a romantic memory. The repeal of the Corn Laws in 1846 had symbolized the waning power of the landed aristocracy, but all classes had shared in the prosperity that followed the "hungry forties." The standard of living of the masses, as well as the level of literacy, had begun to rise and society had become noticeably more law abiding. The millenium that had been sought overnight, first by Robert Owen and then by the Chartists, had been forgotten, but a genuine cooperative movement had successfully taken root and effective trade unions had at last been formed, at least in the more skilled crafts. In these circumstances the middle and upper classes had less reason to fear the extension of the franchise to the working classes. It was still unclear where the lines should be drawn and when the step should be taken, but it may be noted that all the abortive reform bills of the fifties and sixties envisaged a "selective" franchise of the 1832 model on the assumption that there was now a wider range of people qualified to vote. It has been suggested, however, that the arguments used to support this view were too optimistic and that the picture of the working classes painted by the proponents of reform was overly idyllic. As Professor Norman McCord has written in a thoughtful article on the subject, "The process of 'improvement,' though valuable and important, was still very partial and patchy rather than thorough and general in the Britain of 1867." [1]

There is no obvious explanation why the reopening of the question in the middle sixties led to an eventual settlement. A variety of factors helped to produce the necessary impetus—the success of the North in the American Civil War and of Garibaldi and the Italian nationalists in Italy, the pinch of economic distress in England following the

---

[1] Norman McCord, "Some Difficulties of Parliamentary Reform," *Historical Journal*, Vol. X (1967), p. 384.

earlier prosperity, and the renewed agitation led by John Bright (1811–1889) and the newly formed Reform Union (reinforced in 1865 by the more militant Reform League). Perhaps more than anything, the conversion of W. E. Gladstone (1809–1898), now Liberal leader in the House of Commons and the framer of the bill of 1866, pointed to ultimate success. But none of these developments in themselves ensured the final outcome. Although such factors may have had some bearing on political events, in the view of several modern historians, the explanation for the passage of a household suffrage bill in 1867 is only to be found in the development of political events themselves over the preceding eighteen months.[2] Certainly the Second Reform Act that finally emerged was a hit-and-miss affair, not rationally planned.

There were elements in the Cabinet as well as in the Liberal party opposed to the introduction of a reform bill, but Russell and Gladstone forced it on them. Its production was postponed until the necessary statistics had been collected and analysed. The results were surprising and led them to settle on a £7 rental franchise to avoid a working-class majority in the electorate. It was, however, to be tied to occupation and not to ratepaying, thus admitting all those householders, known as "compounders" (i.e., whose rates or local taxes were paid by their landlords), providing they paid at least £7 annual rent. Despite several acts to enable compounders to register as ratepayers, many of them were kept off the registers under the ratepaying provisions of the Reform Act of 1832.

In introducing the bill in the Commons on 18 March, Gladstone launched into a detailed explanation of the provisions but eschewed any attempt to justify it on the ground that the case for reform was so well known.[3] From the beginning it was attacked by dissident Liberals, such as Edward Horsman, Lord Grosvenor, and above all Robert Lowe,[4] who were nicknamed by Bright in a memorable phrase, "the Cave of Adullam."[5] Although the Government nominally had a

[2] See No. 1, p. 75. This is also the view expressed by Maurice Cowling in the Introduction to his *Disraeli, Gladstone and Revolution: The Passing of the Second Reform Bill* (pp. 1–7). J. H. Park in *The English Reform Bill of 1867* (New York, 1920) and Royden Harrison in *Before the Socialists* (London, 1965) pay greater attention to the evidence of extraparliamentary forces.

[3] See No. 2A, p. 79.

[4] See No. 2B, p. 81. Robert Lowe (1811–1892), First Viscount Sherbrooke, had earlier experience of democratic institutions in Australia.

[5] See No. 2C, p. 83.

substantial majority in the Commons, it defeated a hostile amendment of Grosvenor's with very few votes to spare. To meet Grosvenor's nominal objection, a redistribution bill (involving 45 seats) was introduced earlier than had been intended, but despite this conciliatory gesture a second "Adullamite," Lord Dunkellin, moved another hostile amendment, substituting a rating for a rental qualification. This was supported strongly by the Conservative Opposition and passed with 45 Liberals voting in the majority.[6]

Although the Queen urged them to remain in office and Gladstone favored the dissolution of Parliament and an election, on 26 June the Cabinet decided to resign. Lord Derby[7] agreed to form a Conservative ministry, despite his party's minority position in the House of Commons.

The defeat of the Liberal bill and in particular the cutting language used by Lowe in attacking it aroused the latent demand for reform in the country. Throughout the summer and autumn a series of great reform meetings were held, addressed by Bright and other Radical leaders, some of them comparable to the great demonstrations of 1831–1832 in numbers and enthusiasm. The most dramatic and probably the most effective of these meetings was the famous Hyde Park demonstration held on 22 July, shortly after the formation of the Conservative Government, which made the mistake of prohibiting the use of the park in the fashionable West End of London.[8] After registering their complaint to the authorities at the gates of the park, the leaders turned away to hold the meeting in nearby Trafalgar Square; but the great crowd pressing against the railings that surrounded the park found them insecure and easily beaten down. The result was a large-scale scuffle with the police in which a few people were injured and some damage was done to the flower beds. It was a meeting without oratory or order, but it made an impression on the minds of the upper classes that was not forgotten and, taken in conjunction with the numerous other meetings held throughout the country, it undoubtedly influenced events more than some recent historians have been ready to allow.

Shortly after coming into office, Benjamin Disraeli (1804–1881), Conservative leader in the House of Commons, played with the idea

---

[6] See No. 3, p. 89.

[7] Edward Stanley (1799–1869) Fourteenth Earl of Derby, was a one-time member of the Whig Reform Ministry of 1830–1834 and later three times Conservative Prime Minister.

[8] See No. 4, p. 90.

of a quick settlement of the reform question before Parliament was prorogued, but nothing came of the idea. In September it was Lord Derby, supported by the Queen, who revived the issue and Disraeli who was doubtful. In October Disraeli agreed to introduce exploratory resolutions in the House of Commons to see what terms the majority of members might be prepared to support but with no thought of immediate legislation; meanwhile the Queen continued to press Derby to settle the matter.[9] On 31 October the Cabinet unanimously agreed to take up the issue of reform and proceeded to discuss it for the next three months.[10] On 22 December, Derby proposed "household suffrage combined with plurality of voting," and on 6 February the Cabinet decided to include this principle in the resolutions to be submitted to the House of Commons on the 11th; before that date, however, it was abandoned in face of opposition from General Peel.[11] The resolutions eventually tabled set forth the desirability of an increase in the county and borough franchises but warned that it was "contrary to the constitution of this Realm to give any one class or interest a predominant power over the rest of the Community." Consequently they proposed to restrict the vote to ratepayers and to adopt the principle of "plurality of votes" (i.e., second votes for members of the upper classes who had extra educational or financial qualifications).[12]

The resolutions were not well received,[13] and three days later Disraeli committed the Government to legislation without the prior agreement of the Cabinet. On 15 February he sketched the outline of a bill with a £5 borough franchise and plurality of voting, but four days later the Cabinet reduced the borough franchise to include all ratepayers; i.e., "household suffrage." In actual fact this provision would have excluded a large proportion of the poorer householders—the compounders, whose rates were paid by the landlord.

Nevertheless, when Lord Cranborne examined the figures over the weekend he found that they increased the working-class electorate more than he was willing to accept, with the result that a hastily convened Cabinet meeting reverted to a £6 rating bill, which Derby

[9] See No. 5A, p. 91.

[10] See Nos. 5B and C, p. 92.

[11] See No. 5D, p. 93. General Jonathan Peel (1799–1879), a younger brother of the former Conservative Prime Minister, was Secretary for War.

[12] Hansard, vol. 185, Appendix, n.p.

[13] See No. 5E, p. 94.

presented to a party meeting ten minutes later and Disraeli introduced in the House of Commons in the same afternoon.[14]

The bill made a bad impression on the House, and on 28 February a meeting of 150 Conservative back benchers at the Carlton Club urged the Cabinet to revert to household suffrage. This they did on 2 March, although it led to the resignation of the three ministers, Lords Cranborne and Carnarvon and General Peel. On 18 March Disraeli introduced the Conservative Reform Bill based on household suffrage and personal payment of rates,[15] a provision bitterly attacked by Gladstone,[16] who continued his criticism in the debate on the second reading by listing ten major defects in the bill.[17] The bill was accepted in principle on the second reading without a division, on the understanding that it could be amended in committee. There it was turned inside out, mostly as the result of private Liberal amendments accepted by Disraeli, who was determined to see it passed no matter what the form. But the victory did not belong to Gladstone, who failed to keep control of his own party. A group of dissident Liberals, meeting in the Tea Room of the House on 8 April, refused to follow his lead against the Government, some out of personal distrust, others for fear that the passage of the bill would be endangered. Disraeli was ready to accept amendments from back-bench Liberals, and as a result most of Gladstone's original objections to the bill were met. The problem of the compound householder, championed by Gladstone and most of the Liberals, threatened, however, to be the bill's downfall until Hodgkinson, one of the Liberal back-benchers, introduced an amendment requiring all householders to pay their own rates and thus to become ratepayers within the meaning of the bill.

This transformed the measure overnight and for the first time made household suffrage genuine and meaningful. Nevertheless, despite its implications, Disraeli gambled and accepted it in principle without consulting the Cabinet.[18] Although Gladstone would have preferred a less extensive measure, excluding the poorest householders, he felt so strongly the injustice of excluding all compounders, no matter what

---

[14] See Nos. 5F and G, pp. 94 and 95. Robert Cecil (1830–1903), Viscount Cranborne, later Third Marquis of Salisbury, was Secretary for India and subsequently Prime Minister.

[15] See No. 5I and 6A, pp. 97 and 99.

[16] See No. 6B, p. 104. For Gladstone's view of the session see John Morley, *Life of Gladstone* (London, 1903), Vol. II, pp. 223–226.

[17] See No. 6C, p. 105.

[18] See No. 6D, p. 106.

their rent or social status, that he too accepted the amendment, and so, almost by accident, the English boroughs obtained what was virtually a democratic franchise. The franchise in the counties was lowered from £50 to £12 and extended to £5 leaseholders and copy-holders, but this still excluded most of the working classes in the counties. The eventual redistribution arrangements were very limited, although on pressure from the opposition Disraeli slightly increased the representation of the large boroughs. Of the 52 English seats that were abolished for lack of sufficient voters (or, in the case of 7, for corruption) 25 were allotted to counties, 13 to new boroughs, 6 as additional seats to large boroughs, 1 to the University of London and 7 to Scotland.[19] After a final round of bitter denunciations from Cranborne[20] and Lowe, the amended bill passed its third reading in the House of Commons without a division on 15 July.[21] Derby piloted it through the House of Lords successfully,[22] despite the forebodings expressed by most of the speakers, and it finally became law on 15 August. The Commons accepted one amendment from the Lords, limiting electors to two votes in three-member constituencies, with a view to giving representation to minorities. Separate reform acts were passed for Scotland and Ireland in 1868.

During the passage of the Second Reform Act, agitation outside Parliament was not on the scale or of the intensity of 1831–1832, but the Reform League had been active and on 6 May, a week before the Hodgkinson amendment, a mass demonstration was held in Hyde Park in defiance of warnings from the Government. Lord Derby merely acknowledged that the incident created "some slight humilia-tion in the public mind," but historians are divided in assessing the importance of such pressure.[23]

The Reform Act of 1867 had expanded the borough electorate from 600,000 to 1,400,000 and raised the total number of voters from 1,358,000 to 2,477,000. The new voters, however, were very unevenly spread, since the great majority were in the boroughs, most of them in the large urban constituencies. The redistribution was much less extensive than in 1832, while the uneven spread of the new voters further accentuated existing anomalies and, it was hoped, kept the majority of constituencies still manageable. The borough and county

---

[19] See Appendix 3. The final redistribution provisions were only completed in 1868.
[20] See No. 6E, p. 107.
[21] See No. 6F, p. 109.
[22] See No. 6G, p. 109.
[23] See No. 8A, p. 115.

constituencies now differed more radically and the variation in the number of voters in the large and small boroughs was further accentuated.

A majority of the members of both houses of Parliament, prompted by the mixed and often obscure motives that influence politicians, had passed an extensive measure of parliamentary reform that brought Britain a step closer to democracy. Writers in advanced journals such as the *Westminster Review* and the *Fortnightly Review* naturally welcomed the new act, and even the Whiggish *Edinburgh Review* accepted it complacently as a triumph for the Liberal party. Lord Cranborne attacked it anonymously and bitterly in the Tory *Quarterly Review*,[24] Walter Bagehot discussed its consequences gloomily in the second edition of his celebrated book on *The English Constitution*,[25] and Thomas Carlisle assailed it in his vitriolic pamphlet *Shooting Niagara*.

Modern historians, whose interest in the Second Reform Act has been stimulated by its recent centenary, have been more concerned to explain how it came to be passed. Conservative writers, such as Miss Himmelfarb,[26] Mr. Cowling[27] and to a lesser extent Mr. Robert Blake,[28] have played down the element of popular pressure and stressed the creative role of Disraeli, a Conservative statesman, in finding a measure to suit the needs of the time and of generations to follow. Other writers, such as Professor Hanham[29] and Dr. F. B. Smith,[30] have taken a more dispassionate view but recognize the great political and constitutional significance of the act. Its redistribution clauses were much less dramatic than those of the act of 1832, but it went very much further along the road to democracy by its enfranchising provisions.

Lord Derby called the Reform Bill of 1867 a "leap in the dark," and indeed it was, for British politics would never be the same again. Britain was now on the main road to parliamentary democracy and there was no turning back. The majority of members who had voted for the bill would probably have agreed with Disraeli in repudiating

[24] See No. 7A, p. 110.
[25] See No. 7B, p. 111.
[26] See No. 8B, p. 117.
[27] See No. 8E, p. 121.
[28] See No. 8D, p. 120.
[29] See H. J. Hanham, *Elections and Party Management* (London, 1959), pp. ix–xiv and *passim*.
[30] See No. 8C, p. 119.

the idea of democracy, but they had committed themselves to a mass electorate to which party leaders must now appeal. Gladstone set the example in his famous Midlothian campaign of 1880 in which his speeches were addressed to hundreds of thousands of electors far beyond the borders of his rural Scottish constituency, and his words were spread to every corner of the three kingdoms by the cheap popular press that flourished from his earlier removal of the newspaper duties. The mass electorate also required still more elaborate party organization than had sufficed after 1832. Again the Conservatives, spurred by initial defeat on the morrow of reform, took the lead as Disraeli entrusted the task to the able hands of John Gorst (1835–1916), who revamped the party structure from top down. The Liberal response was from the grass roots, or more accurately from the cobblestones of the midland and northern industrial cities, where the genius of Joseph Chamberlain (1836–1914), former Lord Mayor of Birmingham, forged the National Liberal Federation, based on a foundation of elaborate local electoral machines.

There were still, however, many anomalies in the electoral structure, since the Reform Act of 1867 scarcely touched the county franchise and left glaring discrepancies in the distribution of seats. Thus it remained for the reform acts of 1884 and 1885 to eliminate the differential in the franchise between town and county and to bring about the required redistribution.

1
The Climate of Opinion
"Politics and Ideology"

The Reform Act of 1867 was one of the decisive events, perhaps *the* decisive event, in modern English history. It was this act that transformed England into a democracy and that made democracy not only a respectable form of government (the United States was never quite respectable), but also, in the opinion of most men, the only natural and proper form of government. And it was during the debate over this act that the case for and against democracy was most

SOURCE. Gertrude Himmelfarb, *Victorian Minds* (New York: Alfred A. Knopf, Inc., 1968), pp. 333, 338–341. Originally appeared in the *Journal of British Studies* (1966), published by the Conference on British Studies at Trinity College, Hartford, Connecticut. Reprinted by permission of the Conference and the author.

cogently argued. To be sure, the Act of 1867 had to be supplemented by others before universal suffrage was attained. But once this first step was made, no one seriously doubted that the others would follow. The Act of 1867, therefore, more than that of 1832, may deserve the title of the Great Reform Bill. For while 1832 had no necessary aftermath in 1867, 1867 did have a necessary aftermath in 1884, 1918, 1928—the later acts that genuinely universalized the suffrage, not only for Britain but for all those countries that took Britain to be the model of a parliamentary government.

.   .   .   .

By 1865 this habit of apathy that had characterized the preceding decade had become so deeply confirmed that Walter Bagehot made it one of the first principles of the English constitution. He regarded it, however, as a cause for satisfaction rather than for complaint. The "most miserable creatures" in the kingdom, he wrote, "do not impute their misery to politics." Politics to them meant the Queen, and the Queen, they were sure, "is very good." Any agitator who tried to excite political passion would be more likely to be pelted than applauded. "The mass of the English people are politically contented as well as politically deferential." As late as March 1866 Bagehot took this to be the state of the public temper: "There is no worse trade than agitation at this time. . . . A sense of satisfaction permeates the country because most of the country feels it has got the precise thing that suits it."

Exactly three days before this passage appeared in print, Gladstone introduced in the House of Commons the bill that set in motion, as it later appeared, the train of events culminating in the Reform Act of 1867. Bagehot has often been commiserated upon the unfortunate timing that seemed to make his work obsolete even before it had been completed. Yet the fact that his work is so far from obsolete as to be one of our political classics suggests that the events, rather than his words, were somehow amiss. Bagehot, after all, wrote this passage in the full knowledge that a reform bill was imminent: the address from the throne and the speech of the prime minister had left no doubt of this. But like most political observers, he had no reason to think that this reform bill would have a different fate from that of the six other abortive measures introduced in the previous fifteen years—as indeed proved to be the case. What he did not anticipate, what no one anticipated, was that within a year of the rejection of the Liberal bill, another would be passed far more radical than anything that had ever seriously been proposed. (Serious in a practical, parliamentary sense; the Chartists' demands, like those of the Philosophical Radicals earlier, were primarily agitational.) It is this problem that Bagehot's analysis of the English people and constitution forces us to confront: How did an act so unanticipated and unsought, so uncongenial to public and parliament alike, come to pass? Did the "tide of public opinion" change so quickly and powerfully in this short period as to overcome the habitual apathy and traditional deference of the people, and if so, why?

The events most commonly cited by historians to account for such a change in public opinion are the victory of the North in the American Civil War, demonstrating the viability of democracy; the death of Palmerston, making it possible for new principles and personalities to assert themselves; and the economic depression, which inspired demands for political reform. Each of these might fruitfully yield a dissertation in itself. Here it can only be said that, as causes of the Reform Act, they are, singly or together, inadequate to the claims made for them.

The Civil War, for most members of parliament, was more often the occasion for a debater's point than a genuine change of heart toward democracy. A year after Appomattox Gladstone was still complaining of public apathy, and the shifts and turns in parliament during the following year can barely be related to more immediate causes, let alone to an event so far removed in time and place. Even the staunchest reformers were not unambivalent in their reactions to the American experience or in the lessons they drew from it. While one contributor to *Essays on Reform*[1] attributed the vitality of the American government to the strength of democracy, other contributors to the same volume were more concerned with dissociating democracy from the weaknesses and abuses of American politics—dissociating, in effect, the English reform movement from the example of America. The news from America at this time dealt not with the Civil War but with its aftermath: the dissension between the president and congress, bribery at the polls, corruption and peculation among legislators, and the generally low tone of Reconstruction politics—hardly recommendations for the American system.

The death of Palmerston did revitalize politics by producing a void which competing leaders were anxious to fill, but it did not revitalize or encourage new principles. Robert Cecil's description

---

[1] A collection edited by F. Harrison and published in 1867.

of the political mood under Palmerston—"The old antithesis of principle and expediency is absolutely forgotten: expediency is the only principle to which sincere allegiance is paid"—applies even more aptly to the period after his death. Indeed many who witnessed the behavior of Disraeli and Gladstone in 1866–7 came to regard Palmerston as a paragon of principle. Gladstone "unmuzzled" lost none of his old habit of talking out of both sides of his mouth; while Disraeli indulged in his usual freewheeling tactics.

The third factor, the economic depression, is similarly inconclusive. As a major initiating factor in the reform movement, it is ruled out by the simple test of chronology, the Liberal reform bill having been introduced two months before the stockmarket crash and many months before the failure of the harvest. Unemployment and rising prices may have accelerated the movement in its later stages but even then the economic motif was not nearly so conspicuous as might be thought even in the public meetings, still less in the counsels of party and parliament.

The fact is that the actual course of affairs culminating in the Reform Act had little to do with any of these factors. The prospects of reform varied from month to month and week to week (at one point in March 1867, from hour to hour); and these prospects had nothing to do with the triumph of Grant, the death of Palmerston, or the failure of the harvest. Indeed the first passage of arms occurred long before any of these events. It was in 1864 that Gladstone raised the flag of reform with the famous pronouncement that "every man who is not presumably incapacitated by some consideration of personal unfitness or of political danger is morally entitled to come within the pale of the constitution"—followed by the bland assurance that he intended, "of course," no "sudden, or violent, or excessive, or intoxicating change." When his statement was interpreted as an invitation to just such a violent change, Gladstone innocently protested that his reservations about "personal unfitness" and "political danger" could as well be taken to exclude everyone. It was this spirit—reminiscent of the politician who roundly condemns both inflation and deflation and boldly commits himself to a policy of "flation"—that characterized much of the subsequent controversy and made its outcome doubtful until the very end.

2   *The Debate on the Reform Bill of 1866*

(A) W. E. GLADSTONE, INTRODUCING THE BILL, 12 MARCH

[*The following is the conclusion of a very long speech going into the history of parliamentary reform, the complexities of the rating and compounding system, and the recently published statistics on the existing working-class franchise.*]

... I cannot think that even upon the most liberal estimate the present constituency consists of more than 900,000 electors. In addition to those we propose to bring in 400,000, making for England and Wales a total constituency of 1,300,000. The total number of adult males is 5,300,000; so that the whole number enfranchised in town and country would be one in four, as nearly as possible. So much for the figures. I do not know whether the House would like me to recapitulate very shortly the legislative proposals which form the basis of them.

The first is to create an occupation franchise in counties, for houses alone or houses with land, beginning at £14 rental, and reaching up to the present occupation franchise of £50.[1] ... In towns, we propose to place compound householders on the same footing as ratepaying householders. We propose to abolish tax and ratepaying clauses, we propose to reduce £10 clear annual value to a £7 clear annual value, and to bring in the gross estimated rental taken from the rate book as the measure of the value, thus, *pro tanto*, making the rate book the register. We propose also to introduce a franchise on behalf of lodgers, which will comprehend both those persons holding part of a house with separate and independent access, and those who hold part of a house as inmates of the family of another person. The qualification for which will be the £10 clear annual value of apartments, without reference to furniture. ...

Sir, I have detained the House very long in this explanation, and I have now briefly to consider what is the true representation to be made of such a plan as that which we now submit. It certainly makes a

SOURCE. *Hansard's Parliamentary Debates*, third series, Vol. 182, cols. 56–60.

[1] There were also provisions allowing leaseholders and copyholders living in boroughs to vote in the counties and enfranchising savings-bank depositors.

large addition to the constituency. The number of persons who will be enfranchised by this Bill, not upon an estimate wholly vague, but taken on the basis, as far as may be, of the positive and absolute figures which we have been enabled to present, will, I think, certainly be greater than the number of those who were enfranchised by the Reform Act [1832]; for no estimate of the enfranchisement effected by the Reform Act would carry it very greatly beyond 300,000 persons. As respects the county vote, we do not apprehend that it will raise here any question of principle. As regards the borough vote, we hope that our plan is a liberal, as we believe and are sure that it is a moderate and a safe plan. It alters greatly in towns the balance as between the working classes, defined in the liberal manner which I have stated, and the classes above them; and yet it does not give the absolute majority in the town constituencies to the working classes. It is probable that, according to the various tempers of men's minds, we shall be told that we have done too little, or that we have done too much. Our answer is, that we have done our best. We have endeavoured to take account of the state and condition of the country, as well as of the qualifications which the people possess for the exercise of the political franchise. We are mindful that unhappily the limbo of abortive creations is peopled with the skeletons of Reform Bills. We do not wish to add to the number of these unfortunate miscarriages. . . . If we are told that, with respect to the franchise itself, we ought to have done more, our answer is that it was our duty to take into view the public sentiment of the country, disposed to moderate change, but sensible of the value of what it possesses, sensitive with regard to bringing what it possesses into hazard. And, whatever may be the opinion entertained of the growing capacity and intelligence of the working classes, and of their admirable performance at least of their duties towards their superiors—for it has ever appeared to me that though they have sins, in common with us all, yet their sins are chiefly, and in a peculiar sense, sins against themselves— yet it is true of the working classes, as it is true of any class, that it is a dangerous temptation to human nature to be suddenly invested with preponderating power. That is the reason why I think we have not done too little in the way of enfranchisement. We may be told, on the other hand, that we have done too much. I will hope that will not be urged. We do not entirely abandon the expectation that even those who have protested almost in principle against the extension of the franchise downwards will be disposed to accept a measure which they do not wholly approve if they think it offers the promise of

the settlement for a considerable period of a grave, important, complex, and difficult subject. I would beg them to consider what an
immense value there is in the extension of the franchise for its own
sake. Liberty is a thing which is good not merely in its fruits, but in
itself. This is what we constantly say in regard to English legislation,
when we are told that affairs are managed more economically, more
cleverly, more effectually in foreign countries. . . . We cannot consent
to look upon this large addition, considerable although it may be,
to the political power of the working classes of this country as if it
were an addition fraught with mischief and with danger. We cannot
look, and we hope no man will look, upon it as upon some Trojan
horse approaching the walls of the sacred city, and filled with armed
men, bent upon ruin, plunder, and conflagration. . . . I believe that
those persons whom we ask you to enfranchise ought rather to be welcomed as you would welcome recruits to your army or children to
your family. We ask you to give within what you consider to be the
just limits of prudence and circumspection; but, having once determined those limits, to give with an ungrudging hand. Consider
what you can safely and justly afford to do in admitting new subjects
and citizens within the pale of the Parliamentary Constitution; and,
having so considered it, do not, I beseech you, perform the act as
if you were compounding with danger and misfortune. Do it as if you
were conferring a boon that will be felt and reciprocated in grateful
attachment. Give to these persons new interests in the Constitution—
new interests which, by the beneficent processes of the law of nature
and of Providence, shall beget in them new attachment; for the
attachment of the people to the Throne, the institutions, and the
laws under which they live is, after all, more than gold and silver,
or more than fleets and armies, at once the strength, the glory, and
the safety of the land.

(B) ROBERT LOWE, 13 MARCH

. . . Sir, in the course of a long and illustrious career this House
of Commons has gathered into its hands a very large proportion of the
political power of the country. . . .

SOURCE. *Hansard's Parliamentary Debates*, third series, Vol. 182, cols. 141–142,
147–149.

But, Sir, in proportion as the powers of the House of Commons are great and paramount, so does the exploit of endeavouring to amend its constitution become one of the highest and noblest efforts of statesmanship. To tamper with it lightly, to deal with it with unskilled hands, is one of the most signal acts of presumption or folly. When we speak of a Reform Bill, when we speak of giving the franchise to a class which has it not, of transferring the electoral power from one place to another, we should always bear in mind that the end we ought to have in view is not the class which receives the franchise, not the district that obtains the power of sending Members to Parliament, but that Parliament itself in which those Members are to sit, and for the sake of constituting which properly those powers ought alone to be exercised. To consider the franchise as an end in itself; to suppose that we should confer it on any one class of persons because we think them deserving, that we should take it away from one place because it is small, or give it to another because it happens to be large, is in my opinion to mistake the means for the end. . . .

We have to build upon an admission—I cannot extract many principles from the Chancellor of the Exchequer's [Gladstone's] speech, but it is impossible to manipulate figures and statements without implying something—and one thing that he laid down was that he did not wish to see the working classes in a majority in the constituencies in this country; at least, he said he did not much care himself, but for the sake of weaker brethren he would not like to see that. And, therefore, he rejected—with a bitter pang no doubt—the £6 franchise, and took the £7, because the £6 would have given 428,000, which would have been a clear majority of 362,000, whereas the £7 franchise gives 330,000, which leaves a very small majority the other way. . . .

Is it not certain that in a few years from this the working men will be in a majority? Is it not certain that causes are at work which will have a tendency to multiply the franchise—that the £6 houses will become the £7 ones, and the £9 houses will expand to £10? There is no doubt an immense power of expansion; and therefore, without straining anything at all, it is certain that sooner or later we shall see the working classes in a majority in the constituencies. Look at what that implies. I shall speak very frankly on this subject, for having lost my character by saying that the working man could get the franchise for himself, which has been proved to be true, and for saying which he and his friends will not hate me one bit the less, I shall say exactly what I think. Let any Gentleman consider—I have had such unhappy experiences, and many of us have—let any Gentleman consider the constituencies he has had the honour to be concerned with. If you want venality, if you want ignorance, if you want drunkenness, and facility for being intimidated; or if, on the other hand, you want impulsive, unreflecting, and violent people, where do you look for them in the constituencies? Do you go to the top or to the bottom? . . .

The first stage, I have no doubt, will be an increase of corruption, intimidation, and disorder, of all the evils that happen usually, in elections. But what will be the second? The second will be that the working men of England, finding themselves in a full majority of the whole constituency, will awake to a full sense of their power. They will say, "We can do better for ourselves. Don't let us any longer be cajoled at elections. Let us set up shop for ourselves. We have objects to serve as well as our neighbours, and let us unite to carry those objects. We have machinery; we have our trades unions; we have our leaders all ready. We have the power of combination, as we have shown over and over again; and when we have a prize to fight for we will bring it to bear with tenfold more force than ever before." Well, when that is the case—when you have a Parliament appointed, as it will be, by such constituencies so deteriorated—with a pressure of that kind brought to bear, what is it you expect Parliament to stop at? Where is the line that can be drawn? . . .

(C) JOHN BRIGHT, 13 MARCH

. . . I think the world has never shown an instance of a great legislative Assembly such as this making a great disturbance among themselves, exciting themselves, getting into a violent passion, pouring out even cataracts of declamation like that we heard last night, and all upon the simple question whether the franchise in boroughs shall remain as now at £10 or shall be fixed for a time at £7. . . .

The right hon. Gentleman below me (Mr. Horsman) said a little against the Government and a little against the Bill, but had last night a field night for an attack upon so humble an individual as I am. The right hon. Gentleman is the first of the new party who has expressed his great grief by his actions—who has retired into what may be called his political Cave of Adullam—and he has called about him every one that was in distress and every one that was

SOURCE. *Hansard's Parliamentary Debates*, third series, Vol. 182, cols. 212, 219–220, 244.

discontented. The right hon. Gentleman has been long anxious to form a party in this House. There is scarcely at this side of the house any one who is able to address the house with effect or to take much part in our debates that he has not tried to bring over to his party or cabal—and lastly, the right hon. Gentleman has succeeded in hooking the right hon. Gentleman the Member for Calne [Lowe]. I know there was an opinion expressed many years ago by a Member of the Treasury Bench and of the Cabinet, that two men would make a party. When a party is formed of two men so amiable and so disinterested as the two right hon. Gentlemen, we may hope to see for the first time in Parliament a party perfectly harmonious and distinguished by mutual and unbroken trust. But there is one difficulty which it is impossible to remove. This party of two is like the Scotch terrier that was so covered with hair that you could not tell which was the head and which was the tail. . . .

Now, I think if you do not moderate your tone and your views with regard to the great bulk of the working classes, you will find your country gradually weakened by a constantly increasing emigration. And you will find some accident happening when you will have something more to do than you are asked to do to-night, under threats, and it may be under the infliction of violence. Now, Sir, I said at the beginning that I did not rise to defend this Bill. I rose for the purpose of explaining it. It is not the Bill which, if I had been consulted by its framers, I should have recommended; if I had been a Minister it is not the Bill which I should have consented to present to the House. I think it is not adequate to the occasion, and that its concessions are not sufficient. But I know the difficulties under which Ministers labour, and I know the disinclination of Parliament to do much in the direction of this question. I shall give it my support because as far as it goes it is a simple and an honest measure, and because I believe if it becomes law it will give more solidity and duration to everything that is good in the Constitution, and to everything that is noble in the character of the people of these realms.

(D) JOHN STUART MILL, SECOND READING, 13 APRIL

. . . Is there, I wonder, a single Member of this House who thoroughly knows the working men's view of trades unions, or of strikes, and could bring it before the House in a manner satisfactory to working

SOURCE. *Hansard's Parliamentary Debates*, third series, Vol. 182, cols. 1260–1261.

men? . . . I grant that, along with many just ideas and much valuable knowledge, you would sometimes find pressed upon you erroneous opinions—mistaken views of what is for the interest of labour; and I am not prepared to say that if the labouring classes were predominant in the House, attempts might not be made to carry some of these wrong notions into practice. But there is no question at present about making the working classes predominant. What is asked is a sufficient representation to ensure that their opinions are fairly placed before the House, and are met by real arguments, addressed to their own reason, by people who can enter into their way of looking at the subjects in which they are concerned. In general, those who attempt to correct the errors of the working classes do it as if they were talking to babies. They think any trivialities sufficient; if they condescend to argue, it is from premises which hardly any working man would admit; they expect that the things which appear self-evident to them will appear self-evident to the working classes: their arguments never reach the mark, never come near what a working man has in his mind, because they do not know what is in his mind. Consequently, when the questions which are near the hearts of the working men are talked about in this House—there is no want of good will to them, that I cheerfully admit; but everything which is most necessary to prove to them is taken for granted. Do not suppose that working men would always be unconvincible by them. . . .

I believe it will be found that the educated artizans, those especially who take interest in politics, are the most teachable of all our classes. They have much to make them so; they are, as a rule, more in earnest than any other class; their opinions are more genuine, less influenced by what so greatly influences some of the other classes—the desire of getting on; and their social position is not such as to breed self conceit. Above all, there is one thing to which, I believe, almost every one will testify who has had much to do with them, and of which even my own limited experience supplies striking examples; there is no class which so well bears to be told of its faults—to be told of them even in harsh terms, if they believe that the person so speaking to them says what he thinks, and has no ends of his own to serve by saying it. I can hardly conceive a nobler course of national education than the debates of this House would become, if the notions, right and wrong, which are fermenting in the minds of the working classes, many of which go down very deep into the foundations of society and government, were fairly stated and genuinely discussed within these walls. . . .

(E) BENJAMIN DISRAELI, SECOND READING, 27 APRIL

. . . A reduction in the borough franchise is the real cause of the introduction of this Bill, and the real cause of the reduction of the borough franchise is a wish to introduce the working classes to their fair share in the constituent body. . . . The question before us is not whether we are afraid of the working man, but whether we can improve the English Constitution. Now, I hold the English Constitution not to be a phrase, but to be a fact. I hold it to be a polity founded on distinct principles, and aiming at definite ends. I hold our Constitution to be a monarchy, limited by the co-ordinate authority of bodies of the subjects which are invested with privileges and with duties, for their own defence and for the common good; the so-called Estates of the Realm. One of these Estates of the Realm is the Estate of the Commons, of which we are the representatives. Now, of course, the elements of the Commons vary, and must be modified according to the vicissitudes and circumstances of a country like England. Nevertheless, the original scheme of the Plantagenets may always guide us. The Commons consisted of the proprietors of the land after the Barons, the citizens and burgesses, and the skilled artizans. Well, these are elements I wish to see in them, which I wish to preserve, and if necessary to increase; but I wish also to retain the original character of the Constitution. I wish to legislate in the spirit of our Constitution, not departing from the genius of the original scheme. The elements of the Estate of the Commons must be numerous, and they must be ample, in an age like this, but they must be choice. Our constituent body should be numerous enough to be independent, and select enough to be responsible. We, who are the representatives of the Commons do not represent an indiscriminate multitude, but a body of men endowed with privileges which they enjoy, but also intrusted with duties which they must perform. When we had to consider this question in 1858–1859 we had to discover what was the proportion which these skilled artizans, these handicraftsmen of the Plantagenets, possessed in this great scheme. After the best computation that we could make we arrived at the result that they were about one-eighth of the constituent body. That did not seem to us to be enough; and therefore we had to consider how they could be increased to that amount which we deemed was a sufficient propor-

SOURCE. *Hansard's Parliamentary Debates*, third series, Vol. 183, cols. 96–98, 102–103, 112–113.

tion. . . . We believed it was dangerous to reduce the borough franchise. We did not see where it would end if we once commenced to reduce that franchise; and we were of opinion that to reduce it a little would not open an entry into the Estate of the Commons for those whom we desired to see admitted. We, therefore, endeavoured by other means to obtain that result; and by careful calculation we thought we had arrived at those means. . . . The question is have they or have they not a fair proportion of that Estate of the Commons of which they are entitled to be members? I do not say they have. I say that you should inquire—that you should pause—that you should obtain sufficient information, before you make a change; but, above all, that you should act in the spirit of the English Constitution. I think that this House should remain a House of Commons, and not become a House of the People, the House of a mere indiscriminate multitude, devoid of any definite character, and not responsible to society, and having no duties and no privileges under the Constitution. Are we to consider this subject in the spirit of the English Constitution, or are we to meet it in the spirit of the American Constitution? I prefer to consider the question in the spirit of our own Constitution. In what I say I do not intend to undervalue American institutions, quite the reverse. . . . Now, Sir, I have a passage here which I am sure the House will listen to with attention, for it contains the words of one of the wisest men that ever sat in this House. . . . These are the words of Sir George Lewis[2]—

"You may talk of the rudeness of Monarchical Government, but I defy you to point out anything in Monarchy so irrational as counting votes, instead of weighing them, as making a decision depend not on the knowledge, ability, experience, or fitness of the judges, but upon their number."

Now, Sir, these are wise words to be remembered. Sir George Lewis was a great loss to this country; he was a greater loss to the House of Commons; but he was the greatest loss to the Gentlemen opposite. Sir George Lewis would not have built up the constituent body on the rights of man; he would not have intrusted the destiny of this country to the judgment of a numerical majority; he would not have counselled the Whig party to re-construct their famous institutions on the American model and to profit in time by the wisdom of the children of their loins. Sir, it is because I wish to avert from this country

[2] A former Whig minister who died in 1863.

such calamities and disasters that I shall vote for the Amendment of the noble Lord.

(F) W. E. GLADSTONE, SECOND READING, 27 APRIL

At last, Sir, we have obtained a clear declaration from an authoritative source; and we now know that a Bill which in a country with five millions of adult males—["Oh, oh!" "Hear, hear!" *and cries of* "Order!"] Am I to be permitted to proceed? ["Hear, hear!" *and renewed cries of* "Order!"]—and we now know that a Bill which in a country with five millions of adult males proposes to add to its present limited constituency 200,000 of the middle class, and 200,000 of the working class is, in the judgment of the leader of the Tory party, a Bill to re-construct the Constitution on American principles. . . .

Again, Sir, I return to the broad proposition of my right hon. Friend. He says we have no reasons. Perhaps he does not admit as a reason what was stated the other day by the hon. Member for Birmingham, that there have been a hundred meetings—public meetings held in favour of this Bill. I observed, when those words were spoken, that loud murmurs arose on the other side of the House at the mention of the number, and I have not the least doubt of their good faith. I, however, was persuaded that the hon. Member for Birmingham was right, and turning to the Report of the Committee on Public Petitions, I counted the meetings. [An Opposition Member: Got up!] The meetings are "got up!" are they? Then you have your remedy. Do you get up meetings against the measure? It will then be seen whether it is or is not an easy matter to get an expression of public sentiment on which to found your operations. I know not whether they are "got up" or not; if Gentlemen think they are, it is open to them who think so to try the experiment the other way. But this I know, that I counted the petitions presented from public meetings, and signed by the chairmen of these meetings individually, and I found that between the 11th and the 17th of April there were 187 such petitions, besides 500,000 or 600,000 signatures from individuals in favour of this Bill. . . . Has my right hon. Friend, in whom mistrust rises to its utmost height, ever really considered the astonishing phenomena connected with some portion of the conduct of the labouring classes, especially in the Lancashire distress? Has he considered what an

SOURCE. *Hansard's Parliamentary Debates*, third series, vol. 183, cols. 113, 144–145, 148, 152.

amount of self-denial was exhibited by these men in respect to the American war? They knew that the source of their distress lay in the war; yet they never uttered or entertained the wish that any effort should be made to put an end to it, as they held it to be a war for justice, and for freedom. . . . And yet when the day of trial came we saw that noble sympathy on their part with the people of the North; that determination that, be their sufferings what they might, no word should proceed from them that would hurt a cause which they so firmly believed to be just. . . .

You cannot fight against the future. Time is on our side. The great social forces which move onwards in their might and majesty, and which the tumult of our debates does not for a moment impede or disturb—those great social forces are against you; they are marshalled on our side; and the banner which we now carry in this fight, though perhaps at some moment it may droop over our sinking heads, yet it soon again will float in the eye of heaven, and it will be borne by the firm hands of the united people of the three kingdoms, perhaps not to an easy, but to a certain and to a not distant victory.

Question put.

The House *divided*: Ayes 318; Noes 313: Majority 5.

Main Question put, and *agreed to*.

3   *The Defeat of the Liberal Bill of 1866*

GLADSTONE TO QUEEN VICTORIA, 18 JUNE 1866

This evening Lord Dunkellin, seconded by a Member of the Opposition, moved the substitution of rateable for clear annual value as the basis of the Borough franchise.

The effect of the amendment was evidently to limit the enfranchisement conferred by the Bill. Mr. Gladstone stated early in the evening that the Government could not be parties to such a limitation.

The further question was whether the question could be handled as a dry practical and legal question apart from the political objects of the Bill. This would have been quite practicable had there been a

SOURCE. G. E. Buckle, ed., *Letters of Queen Victoria*, second series (London: John Murray Ltd., 1926), vol. I, p. 334. Reprinted by permission of the publisher.

disposition towards it. But the course of the debate too plainly showed the intention of the supporters of the amendment generally to use it as an instrument for restricting the proposed extension of the suffrage. The indication of this disposition was the most marked feature of the debate: in which Mr. Forster, the Solicitor-General, and Mr. Villiers, with Mr. Bright and Mr. Osborne, were the principal speakers on the side of the Government, Sir Hugh Cairns and Sir Robert Peel the most marked among their opponents. In consequence of the tone which prevailed, Mr. Gladstone stated at the close of the debate, that the Government could not engage themselves with regard to carrying on the Bill in the event of an adverse vote.

On the division, the numbers were:

For the Government	304
For Lord Dunkellin	315
Majority for Lord Dunkellin	11

.   .   .   .

4   *The Hyde Park Riots*

SPENCER WALPOLE TO QUEEN VICTORIA, 24 JULY 1866

House of Commons, Tuesday Morning, 1 A.M.   Mr. Walpole presents his humble duty to your Majesty, and regrets to have to inform your Majesty that the Meeting intended to be held in Hyde Park has led to serious, but not he believes to ill-tempered, disorder.

Sir Richard Mayne has just come down to Mr. Walpole at the House of Commons, and from him Mr. Walpole hears that there was assembled between two and three thousand men, that they failed in procuring admission to the Park through the gates, but that the iron-railings and the stone-work in which those railings were fixed were so weak and insecure that some hundreds of yards of them were thrown down, and the mob by such means obtained an entrance into the Park.

Sir Richard Mayne himself has been struck by a brick—cut on the face: and unfortunately the new road furnished stones and other materials ready at hand for pelting the police. Several persons were struck by brick-bats, and Mr. Walpole is grieved to say that he has heard of one death.

SOURCE. G. E. Buckle, ed., *Letters of Queen Victoria*, second series (London: John Murray Ltd., 1926), Vol. I, pp. 359–360. Reprinted by permission of the publisher.

The Park is now quite clear. The mob in the streets were, generally speaking, good-tempered, but the windows in some houses have been broken; Lord Elcho's and Lord Chelmsford's have been specifically mentioned. . . .

5   *The Evolution of a Conservative Reform Bill*

(A) QUEEN VICTORIA TO LORD DERBY, 28 OCTOBER 1866

The Queen has been thinking a great deal, ever since Lord Derby left Balmoral, of the subject on which she had some conversation with him while he was here. As she then told him, she is convinced that, if the question of Reform be not taken up in earnest by her Ministers, with a view to its settlement, very serious consequences may ensue.

The Queen is well aware of the great difficulties which her Government must be prepared to meet, in any attempt to effect this object, and if she can in any way help in surmounting them, Lord Derby and his colleagues may reckon confidently on her best support and assistance.

It seems evident to the Queen, after the failure of so many successive Administrations, which have all been overthrown in their attempts to settle this question, that it never can be settled unless adverse parties are prepared to concede something, and to meet each other in a spirit of mutual conciliation. Nothing would gratify the Queen more than to be instrumental in bringing about such a disposition; and if Lord Derby thinks there is any chance of its doing good—indeed, she views the matter so seriously that she hardly thinks she would be justified in not making the attempt under any circumstances—she is ready to make a personal appeal to Lord Russell and Mr. Gladstone, and other leading members of both Houses of Parliament, and to urge them, by every consideration of loyalty and patriotism, to meet her present Ministers fairly, in an honest endeavour to find out terms of agreement as might lead to a measure of Reform being proposed which would conciliate the support of all moderate men, and afford at least a chance of setting a question at rest, which, while it continues to be

SOURCE. W. F. Monypenny and G. E. Buckle, *Life of Benjamin Disraeli* (New York, John Murray Ltd. and Times Newspapers Ltd., 1928), Vol. II, pp. 191–192. Reprinted by permission of the publishers and the Beaconsfield Trustees.

made a subject of agitation, must act injuriously upon the best interests of the country, and may even threaten the disturbance of its peace and tranquillity.

Lord Derby need not answer this letter at once. He is quite at liberty to consult his colleagues upon it previously, and the Queen relies with confidence upon their patriotism not to allow any feelings of a mere party nature to interfere with their candid consideration of her suggestions. . . .

(B) LORD DERBY TO QUEEN VICTORIA, 1 NOVEMBER 1866

. . . The first meeting of the Cabinet took place on Wednesday last; and the first question which he brought under the consideration of his colleagues was the course to be pursued in reference to the question of Parliamentary Reform . . . but he did not conceal from the Cabinet your Majesty's earnest desire for an early settlement of the question, and, if possible, by your Majesty's present servants: nor the gracious offer which your Majesty made, of the exercise of any personal influence towards coming to an understanding with the principal Members of the late Government, which might lead to a final and amicable settlement of this great question. It will, Lord Derby thinks, be satisfactory to your Majesty to know that it was the *unanimous* opinion of the Cabinet, that whatever might be the difficulties surrounding the question, it could not be ignored, but must be resolutely grappled with. The mode of doing so is under the anxious consideration of your Majesty's servants. . . .

(C) LORD DERBY TO QUEEN VICTORIA, 10 JANUARY 1867

Lord Derby, with his humble duty, submits to your Majesty that, at a meeting of your Majesty's servants held this afternoon in Downing Street, the course to be pursued in respect to the question of Parliamentary Reform was fully discussed, and, subject to your Majesty's approval, finally and unanimously agreed to. Your Majesty's servants

SOURCE. G. E. Buckle, ed., *Letters of Queen Victoria*, second series (London: John Murray Ltd., 1926), Vol. I, pp. 371–372. Reprinted by permission of the publisher.

SOURCE. G. E. Buckle, ed., *Letters of Queen Victoria*, second series (London: John Murray Ltd., 1926), Vol I, pp. 388–389. Reprinted by permission of the publisher.

are of opinion that it was equally impossible to ignore the question, and, with any prospect of success, to bring forward a Bill, to the provisions of which they, as a Government, should be committed; that there existed in the House elements strong enough to defeat any proposal of any Government, but not sufficiently strong to carry any specific plan; and that it was only by gradually feeling the pulse of the House of Commons, and ascertaining how far a community of opinion might be relied on between the moderate sections of both sides, to the exclusion of the extreme democratic party, that an understanding could be arrived at, leading to an ultimate, and, as far as anything can be, a final settlement of the question. They are therefore agreed that the only mode which offers the prospect of a successful issue is to proceed in the first instance by way of Resolutions, which should embody the principles on which the future Parliamentary Representation should be founded. These Resolutions, if adopted, will pledge the House not only to a Reform, but to a Reform based on such grounds as shall leave all details to be dealt with as matters only of degree; and it will then be the duty of your Majesty's servants to point out to the House the various and important subjects on which Parliament stands in need of farther information before they can really form a judgment as to the practical effect of the new Constituency which they are about to establish. For this purpose, one Resolution will pray your Majesty to appoint a Royal Commission. . . .

(D) DISRAELI TO QUEEN VICTORIA, 11 FEBRUARY 1867

The Chancellor of the Exchequer with his humble duty to your Majesty:

The Chancellor proposed to-night the course of the Government respecting Parliamentary Reform. His statement was listened to with interest.

The general feeling of the House may be summed up as that of curiosity. Until the Resolutions have been seen and considered, it would be difficult, and perhaps presumptuous, to foresee the result. The Chancellor, however, is inclined to believe, that the Opposition will be forced to join issue on the Resolutions, and that they will be defeated. In that case, the progress of the Ministry with the question would, with management, be comparatively easy.

SOURCE. G. E. Buckle, ed., *Letters of Queen Victoria*, second series (London: John Murray Ltd., 1926), Vol. I, p. 395. Reprinted by permission of the publisher.

(E) GENERAL GREY TO QUEEN VICTORIA, 12 FEBRUARY 1867

General Grey is afraid that Mr. Disraeli made a great mess of it last night. His speech, as he reads it, was conceived in the most injudicious spirit, going into a perfectly unnecessary history of past Reform Bills, and, rather personally, accusing Lord Russell of having first, in 1859, introduced a Party spirit into discussion on Reform. His explanation of the views of Government respecting the Resolutions themselves was most meagre; and the Resolutions will now go out to the world without the explanation, that should have accompanied them, of what the intention of Government is, if they are passed. In short, a night, as *The Times* says, has been lost for nothing. Mr. Gladstone's speech was moderate enough, but the question, as to what the Opposition will do, is necessarily left to be answered till the fuller explanation which Mr. Disraeli promises is made next Monday week. No one spoke but Mr. Disraeli and Mr. Gladstone, and General Grey does not think it worth your Majesty's while to read more than the summary of the debate given in *The Times*.

(F) LORD CRANBORNE TO LORD DERBY, 24 FEBRUARY 1867

I trust you will believe that it gives me great pain to have to say what I am going to say.

I find, on closely examining the scheme which Mr. Disraeli brought to the notice of the Cabinet five days ago, that its effect will be to throw the small boroughs almost, and many of them entirely, into the hands of the voter whose qualification is lower than £10. I do not think such a proceeding is for the interest of the country. I am sure it is not in accordance with the hopes which those of us who took an active part in resisting Mr. Gladstone's Bill last year raised in those whom we induced to vote with us. I find that, in almost every case, those of our friends who sit for boroughs with less than 25,000 inhabitants (a majority of the boroughs) will be in a much worse condition in consequence of our Bill than they would have been in consequence of Mr. Gladstone's. . . .

SOURCE. G. E. Buckle, ed., *Letters of Queen Victoria*, second series (London: John Murray Ltd., 1926), Vol. I, p. 395. Reprinted by permission of the publisher.
SOURCE. W. F. Monypenny and G. E. Buckle, *Life of Benjamin Disraeli* (London: John Murray Ltd. and Times Newspapers Ltd., 1928), Vol. II, pp. 233–234. Reprinted by permission of the publishers and the Beaconsfield Trustees.

Unable, therefore, to concur in this scheme, I have to ask you to be good enough to summon a meeting of the Cabinet before the meeting of the party to-morrow. Lord Carnarvon, to whom this evening I showed the figures, concurs with me in this request.

At the same time I am bound in candour to say that I do not see my way to an alternative proposal. The error of attempting to frame a Reform Bill during the week previous to its production is one that, in my opinion, cannot be redeemed.

I need not say how deeply grieved I am by any act of mine to cause inconvenience to you. Though I think the abandonment of the policy under which the Queen's Speech was framed was a disastrous step. I would gladly have gone as far as I could possibly do to prevent any embarrassment to the Cabinet. But if I assented to this scheme, now that I know what its effect will be, I could not look in the face those whom last year I urged to resist Mr. Gladstone. I am convinced that it will, if passed, be the ruin of the Conservative party....

(G) LORD DERBY TO QUEEN VICTORIA, 25 FEBRUARY 1867

Lord Derby, with his humble duty, submits to your Majesty, with unfeigned regret, that the Government has been this day on the point of an ignominious disruption, which, however, has been for the time (and, so far as the ignominy is concerned, permanently) averted. This morning at half past eight Lord Derby received, to his astonishment and consternation, a letter from Lord Cranborne to the effect that, on examining the figures with regard to the franchise, he could not concur in the decision of the Cabinet as come to on Saturday; and a quarter of an hour later he received a similar communication from Lord Carnarvon, avowedly after consultation with Lord Cranborne. Lord Derby instantly despatched a messenger to the Chancellor of the Exchequer, who came down at once; and a summons was sent out for a meeting of your Majesty's Servants at 12.30 to be held here, to avoid publicity. The meeting was one of a most unpleasant character; and, up to a quarter of an hour before Lord Derby had to make his statement to the Conservative Party, he believed that he should have to announce the utter disruption of the Cabinet. Lord Cranborne stood out most pertinaciously; Lord Carnarvon would have followed

SOURCE. G. E. Buckle, ed., *Letters of Queen Victoria*, second series (London: John Murray Ltd., 1926), Vol. I, pp. 399–400. Reprinted by permission of the publisher.

him, though reluctantly; and General Peel, who had, in deference to your Majesty's wishes, waived his own objections to secure unanimity in the Cabinet, said, not unreasonably, that, if unanimity could not be obtained, he was absolved from his engagement to remain. The somewhat humiliating result was that *at the last moment*, and to prevent a discreditable break-up, the Cabinet was compelled to assent to a measure[1] far less satisfactory and comprehensive than that which had been proposed. Lord Derby met his friends, as had been arranged, immediately after, and avails himself of the interval of an hour before he goes down to the House of Lords, to put your Majesty in possession of the state of the case. He has made his statement, which has been very well received; but the provoking part of the case is that no part of it was so well received by the Conservative Party, as that which referred to the more extensive plan which Lord Derby had contemplated, and thought it right to state to his friends, but which he found it impossible to carry out in its integrity.

(H) EXTRACT FROM THE QUEEN'S JOURNAL, 27 FEBRUARY 1867

Got to Buckingham Palace at half past 12. Saw Lord Derby, who was in terribly low spirits, speaking of the extreme annoyance and worry he had experienced from what had occurred, and that he feared things were still in a very bad state. He found that the altered proposals had been viewed unfavourably by the Liberals, as well as by all his supporters, and they would not be able to carry such a Bill through, without humiliating defeats. I urged that, if that be the case, then he should part with the 3 Ministers who were causing all this trouble, and reproduce the original measure, which would show the country that he was sincere in proposing Reform. Lord Derby answered that this would no doubt be the boldest course to take, but it might entail dissolution; he would, however, go and see Mr. Disraeli and send him to me in the afternoon. . . .

SOURCE. G. E. Buckle, ed., *Letters of Queen Victoria*, second series (London: John Murray Ltd., 1926), Vol. I, p. 402. Reprinted by permission of the publisher.

[1] This Bill was nicknamed the Ten Minutes Bill, owing to an indiscreet speech of Sir John Pakington's, in which he told his constituents that Ministers had no more than ten minutes to make up their minds as to their course.

(I) DISRAELI TO GENERAL GREY, 15 MARCH 1867

The principle of the Reform Bill is that the franchise should be founded on Rating, and as no test of value seems at all permanent, and new propositions in respect to it are made every year, we arrived at the conclusion, that we would not connect the Borough Franchise with value, but that it should rest on an occupation alone, rated to the relief of the poor, the ratepayer personally paying the rates. We looked upon these conditions, coupled with an ascertained term of residence, viz. two years, as adequate to secure regularity, and general trustworthiness of life.

The number introduced on these conditions will not be so great as the number proposed last year, and proposed on no principle whatever. The figures are instructive, and I give them from the last and most authentic return of the Poor Law Board.

There are in the Boroughs of England and Wales, 1,367,000 Householders of which 644,000 already are enfranchised. There remain, therefore, 723,000 who have not a vote.

Our proposition, that every householder should have a vote who is rated, and pays his rates, in respect of a house, which he has inhabited for two years, would *qualify* 237,000, of whom, after making the necessary and customary deductions for migratory habits, pauperism, etc., would remain 115,000 which would be our addition to the Constituency, but that Constituency would be founded on a principle.

There would remain 484,000 householders, who are not personally rated, but for whom their landlords pay the rates, compounding with the parishes.

Our principle being that the enjoyment of a public right should depend on the performance of a public duty, and which is the best security for regularity of life, we do not give votes to these compound householders, but we provide that any one of them who, by virtue of the Small Tenements Act, and other Rating Acts, has his rates paid, or alleged to be paid, by his Landlord, may, by the powers of our measure, claim to be rated and pay his rates, and then he will accede to his constitutional privilege, and be placed on the Parliamentary Register.

So, under our measure, every one of these 700,000 will be *qualified*, or may *qualify* himself, to be a voter.

SOURCE. G. E. Buckle, ed., *Letters of Queen Victoria*, second series (London: John Murray Ltd., 1926), Vol. I, pp. 407–409. Reprinted by permission of the publisher.

As there is great, but, I think, unfounded, fear of the numbers that may avail themselves of this privilege (my own opinion is that not 50,000 will ever ultimately avail themselves of the provision) we have proposed that one, and one only, of the new franchises shall have the privilege of a double, or rather second, vote; that is to say, any payer of a certain sum of direct taxation shall be a voter for a borough, but he shall not be disfranchised because he happens to be a householder and also pays rates. He votes therefore in respect of taxes, and of rates.

Lord Derby will not consider this a principle of the Bill; but this must only be known to her Majesty and ourselves; he cannot venture to say *that*, as yet, even to his colleagues; but the course of the debate will prove the wisdom of his determination.

The principle of his measure is *bona fide* Rating, as distinguished from the fluctuating rental or value of all previous measures, and in which there is no settlement.

There has been a meeting of his followers to-day, when he addressed them at great length and with great spirit. There were 240 present, and I was glad to see Lord Cranborne among them. He was silent. Sir William Heathcote was the only person, who at all demurred. Mr. Henley spoke strongly in favour of the measure and produced a great effect. Sir John Trollope, Sir John Walsh, Mr. Banks Stanhope, Mr. Laird of Birkenhead, Mr. Graves of Liverpool, Mr. Kendal of Cornwall, in the same vein. These are all representative men. Mr. Kendal represents the National Club and the high Protestant party. I think, after this meeting, that it may fairly be held, that Lord Derby's party will support him as a mass.

Lord Grosvenor has communicated confidentially with us, and says, that if our measure be founded on a real and personal rating, residence, and some compensatory arrangement against the possible influx of Compound Householders, either the dual vote, or some other counterpoise, he will answer for himself and his friends, and he believes that there is sufficient to carry the Government through, if their own party stick to them. Our utmost efforts are now given to this end.

With regard to the distribution of seats, our proposition is moderate, and, though we propose to take away one Member from 23 boroughs, still in the scheme of last year these boroughs were totally disfranchised, and so far as we can judge, they seem, on the whole, to think they have made a good bargain.

I do not count at all on the support of the Radicals; the measure has really no spice of democracy. It will be assailed by them as "reactionary" more likely.

I think we shall be able to make a satisfactory arrangement about the Scotch seats, but I found it impossible to mix them up with the English ones. It we have the opportunity, her Majesty may rest assured, that her wishes in this respect shall be well considered and attended to. . . .

6   *The Debate on the Reform Bill of 1867*

(A) DISRAELI INTRODUCING THE BILL, 18 MARCH

Sir, I rise to ask leave to introduce a Bill further to amend the Laws for regulating the Representation of the People in Parliament. . . . The House of Commons has combined national representation with the attributes of a Senate. That peculiar union has, in our opinion, been owing to the variety of elements of which it is formed. Its variety of character has given to it its deliberative power, and it owes to its deliberative power its general authority. We wish, I repeat, not only to maintain, but to strengthen that character and those functions; and we believe that, in the present age and under the existing circumstances of the country, the best way to do so is to establish them on a broad popular basis. . . . Popular privileges are consistent with a state of society in which there is great inequality of condition. Democratic rights, on the contrary, demand that there should be equality of condition as the fundamental basis of the society which they regulate. Now, that is, I think, a distinction which ought to be borne in mind by the House in dealing with the provisions of the Bill which I am about to ask leave to introduce. If this Bill be a proposal that Her Majesty shall be enabled to concede to her subjects, with the advice and concurrence of her Parliament, a liberal measure of popular privileges, then there may be many of its provisions which will be regarded as prudent, wise, and essentially constitutional. If, on the other hand, it be looked upon as a measure having for its object to confer democratic rights, then I admit much that it may contain may be viewed in the light of being indefensible and unjust. We do not, however, live—and I trust it will never be the fate of this country to live—under a democracy. The propositions

SOURCE. *Hansard's Parliamentary Debates*, third series, Vol. 186, cols. 6–13, 19–25.

which I am going to make to-night certainly have no tendency in that direction. Generally speaking, I would say that, looking to what has occurred since the Reform Act of 1832 was passed—to the increase of population, the progress of industry, the spread of knowledge, and our ingenuity in the arts—we are of opinion that numbers, thoughts, and feelings have since that time been created which it is desirable should be admitted within the circle of the Constitution. We wish that admission to take place in the spirit of our existing institutions, and with a 'due deference to the traditions of an ancient State.

Last year a Bill was introduced with the same object as that which I have risen to ask for leave to bring in to-night—namely, to amend the Laws for the Representation of the People in Parliament. That Bill was avowedly not founded on a principle; it was avowedly founded, as far as I can understand, on expediency. The right hon. Gentleman who was its powerful advocate in this House seemed to me always distinctly to have laid it down, in the course of his argument on the subject, that it was necessary there should be an admission of the working classes into the constituencies; that in accordance with a figure which he had fixed upon he calculated that a certain portion of them would be admitted; but that if another figure were adopted which he named he thought the number admitted would be excessive, and he therefore recommended the first figure as that which, upon the whole, would, he thought, furnish the best and safest solution of the difficulty. His proposal, therefore, involved no principle. . . . A very considerable amount of time was last Session employed in a very unsatisfactory manner, until at length the House took the matter into its own hands, and, in one of the largest divisions which ever took place within these walls, asserted a principle with regard to the borough franchise which was carried by a majority. That principle was that the borough franchise should be founded on rating. . . . I take it that vote of the House of Commons meant this: If you are going to invest men with the exercise of public rights, let that great trust be accompanied with the exercise of public duty. I take it for granted that was what the House of Commons meant. It meant that the being rated to the poor and the paying of the rates constituted a fair assurance that the man who fulfilled those conditions was one likely to be characterized by regularity of life and general trustworthiness of conduct. That is a principle which the House thought ought not to be lost sight of, but should be a *sine quâ non* in the settlement of the borough franchise.

There are in the boroughs of England and Wales 1,367,000 male householders, of whom there are at present qualified to vote 644,000.

There would, therefore, remain unqualified 723,000. In applying the principle of a franchise founded on being rated to the poor, and of personal payment of the rates, we found that out of these 723,000 now disqualified, or rather not qualified, for voting under the existing law, we should at once have had to take away 237,000—that is to say, that beneath the £10 line which now qualifies there are 237,000 persons who are rated to the poor and who pay rates, and who if the law were so changed that value should not be an element would then be qualified to vote for Members of Parliament. Now, if you add these 237,000 persons who are rated to the poor, and who pay their rates, to the 644,000 who are at present qualified, you will find that there would be 881,000 persons, fulfilling the required conditions—that is to say, almost exactly two-thirds of the whole of the householders in the boroughs of England and Wales. There would still remain 486,000, who would not be qualified under these circumstances, because they do not pay rates personally. A great deduction must be made from those 486,000 on account of persons who might claim to pay the rates; but a great amount of those 486,000 persons would still remain without the opportunity of being rated to the poor, because there are certain Acts of Parliament, some of a general and some of a local character, by which the landlord compounds for the rates of his tenants, who, in consequence, are called compound-householders, and most of these are under the operation of the Act with the details of which every Gentleman in the House is familiar—the Small Tenements Act. . . . And the question arises, ought a compound-householder to have a vote? Well, Sir, in our opinion, assuming that the House is of the same opinion, that the foundation of the franchise should be rating and a payment of rates, and that that is adopted by the House, not as a check, as some would say, but, on the contrary, as a qualification, and because it is the best evidence of the trustworthiness of the individual, we have no hesitation in saying ourselves that we do not think that the compound-householder, as a compound-householder, ought to have a vote. But, Sir, we are far from saying that any person who is a compound-householder, from the effects of Acts which have been passed for the convenience of vestries, should be deprived of the opportunity of obtaining and enjoying this right which persons in the same sphere of life may have granted to them, and which, for aught we know, these compound-householders may be equally competent to possess and to exercise. . . . But with regard to the compound-householders, we propose that every facility shall be given to them—that they shall be allowed to enter their names upon the ratebook, to fulfil the constitutional condition to which I have adverted, and then they will, of course, succeed to the constitutional right which is connected with it. Sir, if we pursue that course you have your borough franchise fixed upon principle; you know where you are; you know that the power of electing Members of Parliament must be exercised by men who, by their position in life, have shown that they are qualified for its exercise.

. . . [He went on to propose a vote for the payment of direct taxes and other so-called "fancy franchises."]

Well, I say that if this Bill be carried there is not a man, whether he be a ratepayer paying a rental of less than £10, or a compound householder, who may not qualify himself if he choose. In the new boroughs to which I will afterwards advert the estimated number of voters will be 68,000. The number of direct taxpayers who would probably vote in boroughs will be very considerable. The public departments have no means of offering to the House any recent information upon this subject, and it would probably take months to obtain any. Making due allowance, however, for the increased property and assessed taxes—probably at the rate of 23 per cent—since Mr. Macaulay's Returns were made to the House, I should think that the number who would qualify in boroughs would greatly exceed 200,000. [Mr. Gladstone: From direct taxes.] Yes, from direct taxes. The educational franchise would in the boroughs give 35,000 voters, the fundholders' franchise 25,000, and the savings bank franchise 45,000. You would thus have more than 1,000,000 voters who could qualify themselves in the boroughs for the exercise of the franchise. It has been said that they will not choose to avail themselves of that great right. I regret to hear that opinion, but I venture to doubt its correctness. But still, whatever may be our opinion, it is the duty of the House so to deal with this question that those whom they believe to be qualified for the exercise of this privilege shall have that opportunity, and the duty of Parliament ceases when that has been accomplished.

There is another part of the subject of very great interest, on which, although to-day I am anxious to touch upon nothing but what is necessary, it is requisite that I should make some observations, and that is the distribution of seats. . . . Sir, there are only two courses to follow if you wish to improve the representation of the people by a re-distribution of seats; there is no middle course. You must either create a new electoral map of England, or you must deal practically with the circumstances before you, and follow the line to which I at this moment refer, and which I think the Government has followed. . . .

There is no medium between dealing with the whole question in a vast and solemn manner by means adequate for the settlement of so great a matter, and the prudent, practical method which I mentioned. Well, Sir, we are not prepared to take the first course, although I do not say it is unworthy of deep and respectful consideration; we therefore propose to follow the second, and we have found towns in this country which we think ought to be represented, and whose representatives would bring fresh vigour to this House. The population of the counties, invigorated and vivified with the new franchises which you are giving it, will demand direct representation in this House, and you ought to move in that direction as far as you can, so that counties may no longer be said to be represented only indirectly by small boroughs. . . . We propose, then, that by the thirty seats that will be obtained by the process of disfranchisement we shall give a representative to Hartlepool, Darlington, Burnley, Staleybridge, St. Helen's, Dewsbury, Barnsley, Middlesborough, Wednesbury, Croydon, Gravesend, and Torquay, and two to the Tower Hamlets. In respect to the counties, we propose to divide North Lancashire, North Lincolnshire, West Kent, East Surrey, Middlesex, South Staffordshire, and South Devon, and give them two Members each, and, dividing South Lancashire, also, we propose to give it an additional Member. We also propose to give a seat to the London University.

. . . I hope, therefore, the House of Commons will give this measure a fair and candid consideration. We believe it is one which, if adopted in spirit, will settle its long differences; and that it is qualified to meet the requirements of the country. I am told for certain that there are objections against it; but I beg to remind the House of the distinction which we draw between popular privileges and democratic rights. I am told that in this measure there are checks and counterpoises, and that it assumes in this country the existence of classes. If there are checks and counterpoises in our scheme, we live under a Constitution of which we boast that it is a Constitution of checks and counterpoises. If the measure bears some reference to existing classes in this country, why should we conceal from ourselves, or omit from our discussions, the fact that this country is a country of classes, and a country of classes it will ever remain? What we desire to do is to give every one who is worthy of it a fair share in the government of the country by means of the elective franchise; but, at the same time, we have been equally anxious to maintain the character of the House, to make propositions in harmony with the circumstances of the country, to prevent a preponderance of any class, and to give a representation to the nation.

(B) GLADSTONE, 18 MARCH

While I, of course, fully believe in the good faith with which the Chancellor of the Exchequer gives us the results which he expects from those several franchises, I must entirely decline to accept his figures. Without questioning the right hon. Gentleman's good faith, I look upon those figures as wholly erroneous and visionary. To speak frankly, I look upon three-fourths of the enormous number of voters whom he paraded in different regiments—as 20s. direct taxes men, educational franchise men, £50 fund men, and £50 savings bank men, who are not enfranchised by any other means—this is not a question of dual voting—as little more than men in buckram. My objection is to the estimate of the right hon. Gentleman. The principle of those votes is open to a great deal of comment, which need not be entered upon on this occasion. The vital point is the borough franchise, and to that I will confine the remarks which I feel called upon to make. . . . He says he is going to enfranchise 237,000 persons who are rated to the relief of the poor and who pay their rates; and he insists upon taking the gross numbers comprised in each class, quite irrespective of the fact that some whom those numbers include are on the register already, that others whom those numbers include cannot possibly get on the register because they have not resided and paid rates for the requisite time; and that others whom those numbers include are absolutely incapacitated for being placed on the register on account of their being habitually excused from the payment of rates in consequence of their poverty. . . . Without entering at this moment into any details, I will venture to say that of these 237,000 men, in point of fact not as many as 140,000, when you have made the necessary deductions, will be added to the register. . . . But I was astounded when the right hon. Gentleman descended from the pedestal of the Constitution on which he had seated himself and dealt with the case of the compound-householder. He said that the compound-householder was, after all, as good a man as anybody else; he might be competent to enjoy the franchise and to fulfil his duties as a voter; but as the owner of the property by paying the rates has deprived him of the position which he would otherwise hold, we will, says the right hon. Gentleman, give the compound-householder every facility. The right hon. Gentleman then boldly proceeded to place upon his list of enfranchised citizens 486,000 persons who do

SOURCE. *Hansard's Parliamentary Debates*, third series, Vol. 186, cols. 28–31, 40–43.

not pay rates, but who come under the description of compound-householders. But, if that is so, where is this great principle of the British Constitution? What is the use of talking about the value of rating and setting forth doctrines like that which the right hon. Gentleman propounds when he talks of the completeness and authenticity of this principle? When he talks of the duties which ratepayers have to discharge and which less fortunate members of the community do not discharge? What is the use of setting up a principle in order to knock it down again? . . . Then comes the duality of the right hon. Gentleman; and here alone he was moderate in the computation of his numbers. He did not venture upon a higher figure than 200,000, although he left, I admit, a broad margin beyond. The right hon. Gentleman knows very well—he must know—that there must be many more than 200,000 of these dual votes. . . . To this dual vote, from this moment, be the numbers great or small, I, for one, record an implacable hostility.

(C) GLADSTONE, SECOND READING, 25 MARCH

. . . Sir, it appears to me nothing can be more discouraging than the prospect, when we survey the main heads connected with the settlement of the question. Sketching them lightly, and not attempting artificially to multiply those difficulties, I find they amount to these ten: A Bill on this subject must, I think, to be satisfactory, contain a lodger franchise; but this Bill contains no lodger franchise. It seems to me that a Bill of this kind, professing largely to enfranchise downwards, must provide some means of preventing the traffic in votes that would infallibly arise in a large scheme affecting the lowest class of householders. This Bill contains no such provisions. It seems to me we must do away with the vexatious distinctions that now exist between compound-householders in a condition of life and society that are recognized by law as fitting them for the franchise, and those persons of the very same condition not being compound-householders. This Bill does not do away with these distinctions; on the contrary, it introduces new ones. I think that the taxing franchise must be omitted. I think that the dual vote must be abandoned. I apprehend there is no doubt that the re-distribution of seats proposed by this Bill must be considerably enlarged. I also venture to take it for

SOURCE. *Hensard's Parliamentary Debates*, third series, Vol. 186, col. 475.

granted that the county franchise proposed by the Bill must be reduced. I doubt whether the feeling of the majority of the House will
allow the Government to entertain the important provision for the
optional use of voting-papers. And finally, with respect to the collateral or bye-franchises or special franchises—that, perhaps, is the
best term for them—my opinion, I confess, is that, although on
principle no objection can be made to those franchises, or some of
them, yet, when we come to examine we shall find, as we obtain
acquaintance with the conditions of each proposal, that the advantages continually dwindle, that the obstacles and difficulties continually
multiply, and that there will remain finally either a thin and sterile
residuum, or else they will altogether disappear. . . .

(D) DISRAELI TO GATHORNE HARDY, 18 MAY

I have had great difficulties about the Reform Bill since we parted,
and have terribly missed your aid and counsel.

On Thursday night, Dalgleish gave notice of a motion for Committee
on Compound Householders, which, if carried, would have "hung up"
the Bill, and which, as it was to be supported by all the Independent
Liberals and many of our own men, would certainly have been carried.
I prevailed on him, yesterday morning, to give this intention up, but
he informed us at the same time that he, and all his friends, and many
of ours, as we knew, must support Hodgkinson's amendment for
repeal of Small Tenements Act.

I sent off to you, but you had gone to Osborne: Lord Barrington
told me, however, that you had mentioned to him that you were not
unfavorable to the repeal in itself. I sent for Lambert, who, after long
consultation with myself and Thring, said, if required, he could effect
the repeal of the Rating Bill in five clauses, and was in favor of it. Two
months ago such a repeal was impossible: but a very great change had
occurred in the public mind on this matter. Two months ago Gladstone
would have placed himself at the head of the Vestries and "Civili-
sation". Now, we were secretly informed, he intended to reorganize
on the principle of repeal of Local Acts.

In this state of doubt and difficulty I went down to the House; and

SOURCE. W. F. Monypenny and G. E. Buckle, *Life of Benjamin Disraeli* (London: John
Murray Ltd. and Times Newspapers Ltd., 1928), Vol. II, p. 274. Reprinted by permission of the publishers and the Beaconsfield Trustees.

about nine o'clock, being quite alone on our bench, and only forty-five men on our side, some of whom were going to vote for Hodgkinson, the amendment was moved, and, as I had been led somewhat to believe, Gladstone got up (his benches with about a hundred men) and made his meditated *coup*, which you will read.

I tried to get up some debate, or, rather, I waited for it, for I could do no more, but it was impossible. His "appeal" to me prevented anyone but Bass and Co. speaking, and they were for Hodgkinson. I waited until the question was put, when, having revolved everything in my mind, I felt that the critical moment had arrived, and when, without in the slightest degree receding from our principle and position of a rating and residential franchise, we might take a step which would destroy the present agitation and extinguish Gladstone and Co. I therefore accepted the spirit of H.'s amendment.

(E) LORD CRANBORNE, THIRD READING, 15 JULY

. . . . We are now at the third reading of this Bill. It is impossible to mention those words without feeling how enormously the Bill has changed since it passed its second reading. In no sense is it the same Bill. When it passed its second reading it bristled with precautions and guarantees and securities. Now that we have got to the third reading all those precautions, guarantees, and securities have disappeared. The hon. Member for Northamptonshire, when it was moved that the Bill should be printed, proposed that beside the Bill as it now stands should be printed a copy of the Bill as it was originally introduced. Besides those two I should like to see yet another document, and that is, the demands which were made by the right hon. Gentleman the Member for south Lancashire [Gladstone] on the occasion of the second reading of the Bill. My right hon. and gallant Friend near me (General Peel) said that this was a compound Bill, and that he did not know to whose authorship it was due. I cannot help thinking that if he had referred to the record I have just mentioned—if he had taken the original scheme of the government, and had corrected it by the demands of the right hon. Gentleman the Member for South Lancashire, he would have with tolerable exactness the Bill as it now stands. I mention this because I see with enormous astonishment that the passing of this Bill is spoken of as a Conservative triumph. Now, it

SOURCE. *Hansard's Parliamentary Debates*, third series, Vol. 188, cols. 1526–1528.

is desirable that the paternity of all the strange objects that come into the world should be properly established; and I wish to know whether this Bill, as is generally supposed, is exclusively the offspring of the Government, or whether the right hon. Gentleman the Member for South Lancashire has not had something to do with it? If he has, it follows as an indisputable axiom that it cannot be a Conservative triumph. Now, I heard the demands which the right hon. Gentleman the Member for South Lancashire made on the second reading of the Bill; most of the Members on this side of the House who heard the speech made by the right hon. Gentleman on that occasion thought that it was imperious in its tone, and I do not deny that there was a stringency in the language employed, which could only have been justified by the character of those to whom it was addressed. Imperious language can only be justified by the obsequiousness with which it is obeyed. Now, I have sketched lightly the demands made on that occasion by the right hon. Gentleman. They are ten in number: First, he demanded the lodger franchise. Well, the lodger franchise has been given. Secondly, and this is the only doubtful one, provisions to prevent traffic in votes. Such provisions, however, are to be contained in another Bill, about the probable success of which I know nothing. My impression is that traffic in votes will be one of the results of this Bill. The right hon. Gentleman next demanded the abolition of obnoxious distinctions between compounders and non-compounders. Not only have those obnoxious distinctions been abolished, but all distinctions whatever have disappeared. The fourth demand of the right hon. Gentleman was that the taxing franchise should be omitted. It has been omitted. Fifthly, that the dual vote should be omitted. It has been omitted. Sixthly, that the redistribution of seats must be considerably enlarged. It has been enlarged full 50 per cent. Seventhly, that the county franchise must be reduced. It has been reduced to something like the point at which it stood in the proposal of last year. Eighthly, that the voting papers must be omitted. To my extreme regret, the voting papers have been omitted. The last two demands were that the educational and savings banks' franchises should be omitted. These two franchises have been omitted. ["Question!"] Why, what, Sir, is the question but this? Remember that the history of this Bill is quite peculiar: I venture to say that there is no man in this House of Commons who can remember any Bill being treated in the way that this Bill has been dealt with. No man in this House of Commons can remember a Government who have introduced a Bill of this importance, and who have yielded in

Committee Amendments so vitally altering the whole constitution and principle of the Bill as has been done in the present instance. I think, therefore, it is but fair on the third reading of this Bill, when it appears before us for the last time in a full House, that we should be allowed to trace the changes to their sources that have been made in it. I venture to impress this upon the House, because I have heard it said that this Bill is a Conservative triumph. If it be a Conservative triumph to have adopted the principles of your most determined adversary, who has just come into the House—the hon. Member for Birmingham; if it be a Conservative triumph to have introduced a Bill guarded with precautions and securities, and to have abandoned every one of those precautions and securities at the bidding of your opponents, then in the whole course of your annals I will venture to say the Conservative party has won no triumph so signal as this. . . .

(F) DISRAELI TO QUEEN VICTORIA, 15 JULY 1867

The Chancellor of the Exchequer with his humble duty to your Majesty.

The English Reform Bill passed the House of Commons without a division. House full; the evening began with great bitterness in speeches from Mr. Lowe and Lord Cranborne, but the Chancellor of the Exchequer vindicated the course of the Tory Party amid universal sympathy, and Mr. Gladstone, who had been taking copious notes, refrained from replying.

(G) LORD DERBY, "ON QUESTION, THAT THE BILL DO PASS?" 6 AUGUST 1867

. . . I have felt strongly the necessity and the importance of passing this Bill—first of all because, after being accepted by the House of Commons, its rejection by your Lordships would have been fraught with imminent peril; and next, because I indulged a hope—which I am glad to see has been shared by noble Lords opposite—that in the adoption of this Bill we may find the means of putting a stop to the

SOURCE. G. E. Buckle, ed., *Letters of Queen Victoria*, second series (London: John Murray Ltd., 1926), Vol. I, p. 445. Reprinted by permission of the publisher.

SOURCE. *Hansard's Parliamentary Debates*, third series, Vol. 189, cols. 951–952.

continued agitation of a question which, as long as it remained un-settled, only stood in the way of all useful legislation. No doubt we are making a great experiment and "taking a leap in the dark," but I have the greatest confidence in the sound sense of my fellow-countrymen, and I entertain a strong hope that the extended franchise which we are now conferring upon them will be the means of placing the insti-tutions of this country on a firmer basis, and that the passing of this measure will tend to increase the loyalty and contentment of a great portion of Her Majesty's subjects.

Bill *passed*, and sent to the Commons.

7   The Views of Two Contemporary Critics of the Reform Act of 1867

(A) LORD CRANBORNE ON "THE CONSERVATIVE SURRENDER"

... There was no doubt at all as to the nature of the resistance offered by the Conservative leaders in 1866 to Mr. Gladstone's bill; there was no doubt of the nature of the support they received in doing so. The division which carried them to power was won by the votes of half-a-dozen men. Numbers of those who voted with them on that occasion would have supported any leader and have accepted almost any bill rather than have promoted a measure of household suffrage. The Conservative leaders knew this perfectly well. They were not ignorant of the motives which inspired the enthusiasm with which the eloquence of Mr. Lowe was received, or of the sentiments which animated the majority of the speeches delivered from their own side of the House. Both in public and in private they were stimulating those feelings to the utmost of their power. Not a single hint escaped from any of them which could damp the ardour of their anti-democratic supporters and allies. By every means at their command they not only allowed but encouraged and sanctioned the belief that they were resisting as excessive the admission of the lower classes to the fran-chise, proposed in Mr. Gladstone's bill. Their supporters were fully hoodwinked. They voted in blind reliance on the assurances they had

SOURCE. Anonymous, in the *Quarterly Review*, Vol. 123 (October 1967), American edition, pp. 283–284.

received. In order to defeat a proposal which they feared might ultimately result in household suffrage, they ousted Mr. Gladstone from power; and when they greeted that victory with tumultous applause, no presentiment crossed a single mind of the utter ruin of their hopes and their cause which by that very victory they had accomplished.

. . . In what terms will the calm judgment of posterity estimate the manœuvres of the successful politicians? If they wish to seek for an historical parallel, they will have to go far back in our annals. They will find none during the period for which parliamentary government has existed. Neither the recklessness of Charles Fox, nor the venality of Henry Fox, nor the cynicism of Walpole will furnish them with a case in point. They will have to go back to the time when the last Revolution was preparing—to the days when Sunderland directed the councils and accepted the favours of James, while he was negotiating the invasion of William.

But it is said on their behalf that the offence was condoned because the party pushed them on. The assertion has undoubtedly been frequently made. It was advanced with especial emphasis by Mr. Disraeli in his speech on the third reading, in which he represented the country gentlemen behind him as a band of buoyant and untameable Reformers who were perpetually dragging old-fashioned Conservatives like himself somewhat faster than they cared to go. The description was humorous; but it was purely an effort of imagination. There was no general expression of opinion on the part of the Conservative party in favour of the bill. Nothing was more remarkable than their general silence in the debates. No division, indeed, was taken against the bill, because, the Liberal party having decided to support it, the Ministers would have obtained with their aid an overwhelming majority. . . .

(B) WALTER BAGEHOT IN THE INTRODUCTION TO THE SECOND (1872) EDITION OF *THE ENGLISH CONSTITUTION*

As I have endeavoured to show in this volume, the deference of the old electors to their betters was the only way in which our old system could be maintained. . . .

The grave question now is, How far will this peculiar old system

SOURCE. Walter Bagehot. Introduction to the Second Edition (1872), *The English Constitution* (London, n.d.; reprint, 1910), pp. 14–17, 24–26.

continue and how far will it be altered? I am afraid I must put aside at once the idea that it will be altered entirely and altered for the better. I cannot expect that the new class of voters will be at all more able to form sound opinions on complex questions than the old voters. There was indeed an idea—a very prevalent idea when the first edition of this book was published—that there then was an unrepresented class of skilled artizans who could form superior opinions on national matters, and ought to have the means of expressing them. We used to frame elaborate schemes to give them such means. But the Reform Act of 1867 did not stop at skilled labour; it enfranchised unskilled labour too. And no one will contend that the ordinary working man who has no special skill, and who is only rated because he has a house, can judge much of intellectual matters. The messenger in an office is not more intelligent than the clerks, not better educated, but worse; and yet the messenger is probably a very superior specimen of the newly enfranchised classes. The average can only earn very scanty wages by coarse labour. They have no time to improve themselves, for they are labouring the whole day through; and their early education was so small that in most cases it is dubious whether, even if they had much time, they could use it to good purpose. We have not enfranchised a class less needing to be guided by their betters than the old class; on the contrary, the new class need it more than the old. The real question is, Will they sumbit to it, will they defer in the same way to wealth and rank, and to the higher qualities of which these are the rough symbols and the common accompaniments?

There is a peculiar difficulty in answering this question. Generally, the debates upon the passing of an Act contain much valuable instruction as to what may be expected of it. But the debates on the Reform Act of 1867 hardly tell anything. They are taken up with technicalities as to the ratepayers and the compound householder. Nobody in the country knew what was being done. I happened at the time to visit a purely agricultural and conservative county, and I asked the local Tories, "Do you understand this Reform Bill? Do you know that your Conservative Government has brought in a Bill far more Radical than any former Bill, and that it is very likely to be passed?" The answer I got was, "What stuff you talk! How can it be a Radical Reform Bill? Why, *Bright* opposes it!" There was no answering that in a way which a "common jury" could understand. The Bill was supported by *The Times* and opposed by Mr. Bright; and therefore the mass of the Conservatives and of common moderate people, without distinction of party, had no conception of the effect. They said it was "London nonsense" if you tried to explain it to them. The nation indeed generally looks to the discussions in Parliament to enlighten it as to the effect of Bills. But in this case neither party, as a party, could speak out. Many, perhaps most of the intelligent Conservatives, were fearful of the consequences of the proposal; but as it was made by the heads of their own party, they did not like to oppose it, and the discipline of party carried them with it. On the other side, many, probably most of the intelligent Liberals, were in consternation at the Bill; they had been in the habit for years of proposing Reform Bills; they knew the points of difference between each Bill, and perceived that this was by far the most sweeping which had ever been proposed by any Ministry. But they were almost all unwilling to say so. They would have offended a large section in their constituencies if they had resisted a Tory Bill because it was too democratic; the extreme partizans of democracy would have said, "The enemies of the people have confidence enough in the people to entrust them with this power, but you, a 'Liberal,' and a professed friend of the people, have not that confidence; if that is so, we will never vote for you again. . . . "

In one minor respect, indeed, I think we may see with distinctness the effect of the Reform Bill of 1867. I think it has completed one change which the Act of 1832 began; it has completed the change which that Act made in the relation of the House of Lords to the House of Commons. As I have endeavoured in this book to explain, the literary theory of the English Constitution is on this point quite wrong as usual. According to that theory, the two Houses are two branches of the Legislature, perfectly equal and perfectly distinct. But before the Act of 1832 they were not so distinct; there was a very large and a very strong common element. By their commanding influence in many boroughs and counties the Lords nominated a considerable part of the Commons; the majority of the other part were the richer gentry— men in most respects like the Lords, and sympathising with the Lords. Under the Constitution as it then was the two Houses were not in their essence distinct; they were in their essence similar; they were, in the main, not Houses of contrasted origin, but Houses of like origin. The predominant part of both was taken from the same class—from the English gentry, titled and untitled. By the Act of 1832 this was much altered. The aristocracy and the gentry lost their predominance in the House of Commons; that predominance passed to the middle class, The two Houses then became distinct, but then they ceased to be co-equal. The Duke of Wellington, in a most remarkable paper, has explained what pains he took to induce the Lords to submit to their new position, and to submit, time after time, their will to the will of the Commons.

The Reform Act of 1867 has, I think, unmistakably completed the effect which the Act of 1832 began, but left unfinished. The middle class element has gained greatly by the second change, and the aristocratic element has lost greatly. If you examine carefully the lists of members, especially of the most prominent members, of either side of the House, you will not find that they are in general aristocratic names. Considering the power and position of the titled aristocracy, you will perhaps be astonished at the small degree in which it contributes to the active part of our governing assembly. The spirit of our present House of Commons is plutocratic, not aristocratic; its most prominent statesmen are not men of ancient descent or of great hereditary estate; they are men mostly of substantial means, but they are mostly, too, connected more or less closely with the new trading wealth. The spirit of the two Assemblies has become far more contrasted than it ever was.

The full effect of the Reform Act of 1832 was indeed postponed by the cause which I mentioned just now. The statesmen who worked the system which was put up had themselves been educated under the system which was pulled down. Strangely enough, their predominant guidance lasted as long as the system which they created. Lord Palmerston, Lord Russell, Lord Derby, died or else lost their influence within a year or two of 1867. The complete consequences of the Act of 1832 upon the House of Lords could not be seen while the Commons were subject to such aristocratic guidance. Much of the change which might have been expected from the Act of 1832 was held in suspense, and did not begin till that measure had been followed by another of similar and greater power.

8   *Some Modern Views of the Reform Act of 1867*

(A) ROYDEN HARRISON ON "THE STRANGE SYNDROME OF THE LABOUR ARISTOCRACY"

... Party rivalries and calculations were important, but such rivalries and calculations all depended upon the stage of development attained by the Labour Movement. Unless a synthesis is made between the "party conflict" and "class struggle" interpretations, the history of 1866–1867 is unintelligible. Unlike the Chartist years, the agitation of 1866–1867 had a character which allowed the leaders of the traditional parties to think of Reform in terms of what might be "in it" for them. Unlike the years of the abortive Reform Bills, there was an agitation which could only be ignored at the cost of reviving and sharpening the class-consciousness of the workmen and helping on the formation of revolutionary forces.

In the 1860s the British working class exhibited certain "contradictory" characteristics. If it was increasingly "respectable", it was increasingly well organized. If it had abandoned its revolutionary ambitions, it had not wholly lost its revolutionary potentialities. It left no doubt that these potentialities might be speedily developed if it was too long thwarted in its desire to secure political equality. In short, it had attained precisely that level of development at which it was safe to concede its enfranchisement and dangerous to withhold it. It was this circumstance, rather than the death of Palmerston, which determined the timing of Reform.

Professor Briggs has attempted the kind of synthesis which is required. He makes a distinction between the *timing* of events and their *pattern*. Unlike Lowes Dickinson and Herrick he finds room for the Reform League. . . .

. . . There can be no question about the fact that the mysterious nature of Disraeli's genius made its contribution to the passing of the Reform Act. The problem is how far he should be regarded as the master, rather than as the not unwilling prisoner, of circumstance. It is certain that for a number of years Disraeli had sensed that there might be a possibility of using a section of the non-electors to help restore the fortunes of his Party. As the prospect of restoring the

SOURCE. Royden Harrison, *Before the Socialists* (London: Routledge & Kegan Paul Ltd.; Toronto: University of Toronto Press, 1965), pp. 133–136. Reprinted by permission of the publishers and the author.

old Toryism faded, the preoccupation with ending a prolonged period of Whig supremacy grew. He had never had scruples against using the Radicals to further his own ends. But Disraeli's skill at self-advertisment has encouraged his vague premonitions to be treated as if they were cold calculations. Ideas which were half-formed or slowly maturing were taken for developed aims and a clear cut strategy.

Those who try to make the history of Reform intelligible in terms of Disraeli's skill and cunning are inclined to forget that, in the first months of the Tory Ministry, he was not at all anxious to deal with the question and had to be convinced by the Queen and Lord Derby that it was imperative. There is a tendency to overlook the fact that he was forced to make up his mind about important amendments on the spur of the moment. He and Derby frequently talked with a flippancy which is only possible for men who have surrendered to events. . . .

The strength of the Government lay, not so much in the weakness and division of the Opposition, as in the fact that a Reform Act had become essential. A great majority in the House was brought to the conclusion that the whole institution of Parliamentary government would be discredited and imperilled by yet another false start. Had it not been for this consideration then Disraeli could never have carried so many members of his own party with him. Peel, Carnarvon and Cranborne would have become the leaders of a Tory 'cave.' All the Adullamites would have followed Lowe in offering a continued resistance. The Radicals, many of whom were uneasy about the extent of the measure as well as its supposed paternity, would have made it their first interest to defeat the Government.

The largely forgotten events of 6 May throw light on the character of the challenge with which the Government had to deal. When it allowed a reformist movement to score a revolutionary triumph, it showed that it understood the choice before it. A humiliation had been suffered; a humiliation which gave notice that henceforth "good will" rather than "force" or "fraud" was to be the main instrument. It was in accordance with the curious dialectic of the British Political System that it was able to make a strength of its weakness. It exchanged the associations of Peterloo for those of Hyde Park. After 6 May Hyde Park gradually became an established tradition. It stood for freedom in relation to the pretensions of aristocratic privilege, but it also stood for the powerlessness of democratic enthusiasts in the face of those "occult and unacknowledged forces which are not dependent upon any legislative machinery."

(B) GERTRUDE HIMMELFARB IN *VICTORIAN MINDS*

In its initial impulse . . . the creed known as Tory Democracy was latitudinarian rather than democratic per se. But latitudinarianism generated and accelerated the movement toward democracy. What was possible soon became probable and what was permitted became prescriptive. One member of the cabinet noted in his diary at the time that the government was following a "laissez-aller system," yielding and adopting anything in the spirit of "in for a penny, in for a pound." The expression was particularly apt, since it was literally pennies and pounds that were being frittered away. If there was no "hard and fast line" to abide by, no good reason to fix the franchise at any particular point, this itself became reason for fixing it at no point. Disraeli himself explained that, confronted with a multitude of schemes proposing to fix the franchise at "£8, £7, £6, and all sorts of pounds," he had come to the conclusion that there was no "sound resting-place" other than household suffrage. As theological latitudinarianism had been impelled toward rationalism, so political latitudinarianism was now impelled toward democracy.

But there was an additional impetus toward democracy in the Tory creed. This came from the belief that the lower classes were not only naturally conservative in temperament but also naturally Conservative in politics. Thus the party had a practical interest in democracy. The Tories were democratic, one might say, because they assumed that the demos was Tory. . . .

Gladstone's failure of imagination came from a crucial and characteristically Liberal failure of nerve. Lacking the Conservative's faith in the eternal verities of human nature and society, the Liberal had nothing to sustain him but the precarious arrangements of politics. And these political arrangements were all the more precarious because they were entirely and eternally at the mercy of a mass of individuals— as many individuals as there were electors. Each of these individuals was presumed to be independent of and equal to every other; each was presumed to be pursuing his private interests at the expense of everyone else's interests; and each was presumed to be exercising the maximum amount of power available to him so as to achieve the

SOURCE. Gertrude Himmelfarb, *Victorian Minds* (New York: Alfred A. Knopf, Inc., 1968), pp. 333, 338–341. Originally appeared in the *Journal of British Studies*, Vol. VI (1966), published by the Conference on British Studies at Trinity College, Hartford, Connecticut. Reprinted by permission of the Conference and the author.

maximum satisfaction of his interests. To the Liberal, therefore, the political enterprise was eminently serious and perilous. He had to consider every reform carefully and calculate its effect, since any change in the composition of the electorate, any alteration in the political order, might jeopardize the entire structure of society. Unlike the Conservative with his cavalier "in for a penny, in for a pound" attitude, the Liberal had to take account of every penny and every pound. . . .

It is important to insist upon these ideological and temperamental distinctions because they help explain what is surely at the heart of the matter: that the Reform Act was a Conservative measure, initiated and carried by a Conservative government. There was much truth in Gladstone's charge that the Conservatives were less interested in the particular form of the act than in taking credit for passing it. The fact remains, however, that it did take the form it did and that the Conservatives passed it in that form, whereas Gladstone and much of his party were to the end unreconciled to it in that form and agreed to its passage, as Gladstone admitted, only as one would agree to have one's leg cut off to save one's life—literally, to avoid committing political suicide. . . .

. . . . .

The situation, then, was infinitely complicated. And it was made all the more complicated by the fact that although there was seldom a clear economic mandate or compelling interest for this or that policy, there was what might be called an "ideology" of interests. However confused or conflicting their own interests, motives, or policies might be, most Liberals shared the utilitarian philosophy of self-interest, according to which all men were seeking a maximum realization of their interests by means of a maximum utilization of their power. It is this ideology of interests, more than any particular set of interests, that united the various factions of Liberals and distinguished them from the Conservatives. While Gladstone, Lowe, and Bright were trying to calculate the precise effect of this or that reform, on the assumption that each measure of reform would bring into play a measurable interest and power, the Conservatives, having no such utilitarian conceptions, had no need of such calculations. Tory landlords were as vulnerable as Whig landlords—or even Liberal manufacturers—to attacks upon land, property, primogeniture, the currency, and the like. But they worried less about them because they did not believe the masses to be covetous of property, privilege, or power. Indeed, the Conservatives assumed that the masses identified themselves, both in interest and in power, with their betters, that economic advantage or political strength counted less in their order of values than established traditions and authorities. . . .

(C) F. B. SMITH IN *THE MAKING OF THE SECOND REFORM BILL*

The Reform Bill of 1867 survived because a majority of the members of both Houses of Parliament dared not throw it out. They did not want it, they did not like it, they feared what it might do, but they passed it. For the first time in the Second Reform period a majority of members felt an imperative need to make a settlement.

There were three new elements in the situation which decisively swung the balance of forces in the House of Commons. The first was the mass agitation which had sprung up after the defeat of the Liberal Bill, and which kept up its importunity until the borough suffrage provisions of the Conservative Bill were transformed and safe. The second was Disraeli's resolve to carry the Reform Bill, *a* Reform Bill, to consolidate his leadership and to humiliate Gladstone. His determination to cling to the Bill neutralized the traditional Conservative opposition to any wide-ranging Reform and left the Whigs without their natural allies against the radicals. The third element was latent throughout the period, but it only wreaked its full havoc in 1867. It was the mixture of boredom and confused disillusionment that set in as some of the members gradually realized, during the interminable debates on the rating laws, that the safe, limited enfranchisement of the artisan élite was a fantasy appropriate only to those dear, dead days when Reform was not urgent. The central themes of the long and brilliant debate of the period, the worth of the artisans and the machinery for effecting their admittance, gradually faded into irrelevance.

The collapse of the borough qualification was inevitable from the time that Disraeli decided, in his ignorance, to use "personal payment" as the restrictive mechanism. It worked brilliantly as a political ruse, for it deceived his own supporters and made Gladstone appear a humbug when he tried to explode it. But Disraeli, with a minority behind him, could not impose his will on the House in the shaping of the Bill: instead, he could only play on the Liberals' distrust of Gladstone, on their dread of further agitation and on their fears of a dissolution.

SOURCE. F. B. Smith, *The Making of the Second Reform Bill* (Cambridge: Cambridge University Press, 1966), pp. 229–230. Reprinted by permission of the publisher.

He was helped by the agitations, which quickened the need for a settlement and reduced the details of the Bills to petty-seeming hindrances.
Whenever Gladstone sought to grapple with the technical difficulties
in the measures, to ensure that they would fulfill their ostensible
purpose of a restrictive Reform, Disraeli could isolate him by claiming
that he was trying to obstruct a settlement. The great changes in the
Bill—the lodger franchise, Hodgkinson's amendment, the enlarged
redistribution—were all made after a minimum of debate, and the first
two without even a division. Disraeli led his country gentlemen to
accept anything as long as they appeared to be winning. The acceptance of Reform by the country gentlemen reflected their underlying
confidence in the submissiveness of the workingmen—a confidence
founded on the economic and social stability of the previous eighteen
years.

Lowe's arguments against "democracy" had been a powerful
stimulus to those Whigs and Tories who had joined to smash the Bill
of 1866, but that success makes the Adullamites' ineffectiveness in
1867 all the more striking. Apart from the amendment instituting a
cumulative voting arrangement in the "triangular" constituencies,
the Opposition case of 1866 would seem to have been forgotten. It
was forgotten, midst the haste to find a settlement, because Disraeli
took over the Reformers' arguments and used them to isolate the
Adullamite and Tory incorruptibles, and thereby induce his bemused
country gentlemen to swallow the Liberals' amendments.

(D) ROBERT BLAKE IN *DISRAELI*

It is probably true that the Reform Bill did in the end enfranchise
a class which for a number of reasons tended to vote Conservative
rather than Liberal. It is also true that Disraeli, more than any
other statesman of his day, had the imagination to adapt himself to
this new situation and to discern, dimly and hesitantly perhaps,
what the artisan class wanted from Parliament. Imperialism and
social reform were policies which certainly appealed to them—or to
a large section of them—and Disraeli seems to have sensed this in
his curiously intuitive way, although even here it is important not
to overstate the case. But there is nothing—or very little—to suggest

SOURCE. Robert Blake, *Disraeli*: (London: Eyre & Spottiswoode Ltd., 1967), p. 477.
Reprinted by permission of the publisher and the author.

that he had any such awareness in 1867. The importance of that period in his life is quite different. In the course of two years from the summer of 1865 he transformed his position in the Conservative party. It was his sparkling success in the session of 1867 which made him, as he had by no means been before, Derby's inevitable successor. In this respect as a stage in his career the session of 1867 can only be compared to that of 1846. For, whatever Cranborne and his exiguous "Cave" might say—and they said much very acidly—the party as a whole was dazzled by his sheer parliamentary skill. They loved the sense of victory which he gave them; it was a feeling they had not had for years, some of them never before. And they were with a few exceptions so delighted to see the question settled over the heads of the official opposition that they blinded themselves to the magnitude of the concessions made to the Radicals. It was like a moonlight steeplechase. In negotiating their fences few of them saw where they were going, nor much cared so long as they got there first.

No one could exploit this mood more effectively than Disraeli. For him, too, it was an exciting sport, a race requiring steady hands, good nerves and plenty of courage. He was a master at disguising retreat as advance. Of Disraeli at this time it could be said as Lord Beaverbrook wrote of Lloyd George: "He did not seem to care which way he travelled providing he was in the driver's seat." For what he did in 1867 he deserves to go down to history as a politician of genius, a superb improviser, a parliamentarian of unrivalled skill, but not as a far-sighted statesman, a Tory democrat or the educator of his party.

(E) MAURICE COWLING IN *DISRAELI, GLADSTONE AND REVOLUTION: THE PASSING OF THE SECOND REFORM BILL*

. . . What conclusion do we draw? There was no "capitulation" to popular pressure. The Conservative party was not overborne by Beales and Bright. Disraeli did not revert to being a Radical. Derby did not suddenly discover Marx. Since there was to be a predominantly working-class electorate in the boroughs, they had to put themselves right with it, just as Lord John Manners expected Master

SOURCE. Maurice Cowling, *Disraeli, Gladstone and Revolution: The Passing of the Second Reform Bill* (Cambridge: Cambridge University Press, 1967), p. 310. Reprinted by permission of the publisher and the author.

and Servant legislation to "put" them "right with the working classes" among the old electorate. The result was a Tory social policy in the 'seventies. But what Derby and Disraeli were imitating in 1867 was Palmerston or Peel, and until March 1867 more Palmerston in his most conservative phase than anything else. There was nothing inevitable about the course they followed. If a restrictive Act could have been passed on a conservative basis, they would have passed it. If party conditions had been suitable, they would have persisted in March 1867 with a restrictive proposal, and would have appealed to the existing electorate if defeated on it. But the Cave's reluctance, Whig refusals and Disraeli's preferences had destroyed the chance of comprehensive resistance in July 1866. The consequence was a minority government and disjointed resistance in February 1867. Once he had been ousted on the more conservative line, Disraeli staked out his own. Just as Russell and Gladstone had to agree to immediate legislation in 1865–1866 since they could get Forster to join the government and not Stanley, and adopted a more radical line because they were compelled to by the Cave's resistance, so the Cave/Cranborne resistance in 1867 drove Derby and Disraeli to greater concession than they may otherwise have intended. It was not the weakness of conservative feeling in the House of Commons which drove Disraeli this way, but the fact that Radical demands were not too extensive to be met and the obstacle he, among others, presented to any attempt to give viable party shape to a policy of resistance. If a united Conservative Cabinet had led the way on February 25 1867, it could have formed the nucleus of an unbeatable party. In the divided condition of February 26, it opened itself to any wind that blew.

PART III

The Reform Acts of 1884–1885

INTRODUCTION

Although it was a long time in coming, the Reform Act of 1867 was a natural sequel to the act of 1832. Indeed, as we have seen, it probably went further than the majority of members of Parliament really desired. The next reform of the franchise, however, came much sooner and faced much less resistance. By the 1880s the large addition of working-class voters to the electorate seemed much less dangerous than it had in 1866–1867. Their influence on Parliament was minimal and only one or two of them had been elected to a body of 658 members. Consequently even the Conservative Opposition was not greatly frightened when it was suggested in 1884 that an end should be put to the anomaly that prevented agricultural and industrial workers who happened to live outside the arbitrary boundaries of the borough constituencies from exercising the franchise.

Reformers had always professed to be concerned with seeking to eliminate the corrupt practices that had characterized British elections since the eighteenth century and earlier, but neither the Reform Act of 1832 nor that of 1867 had done very much directly to improve the situation. Indeed, if anything, it had deteriorated after 1832, for all too many of the much-touted £10 householders were found to be venal in the days of open elections and small constituencies. A number of anticorruption acts were passed in the years between 1832 and 1867, but none of them was entirely effective. The great enlargement of the number of voters in many constituencies by the Reform Act of 1867 reduced the possibilities for corruption, as did the Ballot Act of 1872, which was passed in the face of strong opposition from the Conservative party and the House of Lords. This was followed in 1883 by the most effective Corrupt Practices Act of the century, which finally brought the outstanding problem under control by the rigid curtailment of election expenses. Such reforms were, however, subsidiary to the further reform of the franchise and the further redistribution of seats. This was first proposed in the

House of Commons by Charles Trevelyan, then a private Liberal member, in 1876 and again in 1877. On the latter occasion Lord Hartington (1833–1908), who had temporarily succeeded Gladstone as Liberal leader in the Commons, gave the motion his support. The Liberal party was committed to legislation when it formed a government under Gladstone after winning the election of 1880, but the pressure was not overwhelming; other problems loomed large and few were anxious for an early settlement that would require the dissolution of Parliament and a new election. In other words it was generally thought that parliamentary reform might be left until a later session, since, if it was a major measure, it would render the existing Parliament moribund. By 1883 the Radical supporters of the Government were becoming restive and their most effective spokesman, Joseph Chamberlain, who had forced his way into the Cabinet in 1880, began to press the issue in public speeches.[1] More than four hundred public meetings in favour of reform had been held by March 1884. Despite his acceptance of the principle, Lord Hartington fought a delaying action in the Cabinet, especially against the inclusion of Ireland. The majority of his colleagues, however, believed it could not be put off any longer and on 4 January 1884 agreed on the terms of a bill,[2] which Gladstone introduced into the House of Commons on 28 February. The bill proposed to add almost two million voters by extending household suffrage to the counties throughout the United Kingdom;[3] it also retained the other qualifications of preceding acts, and thus made it possible for property holders to have more than one vote. Gladstone refused to overload the bill by including clauses on redistribution, which he preferred to leave for the following session. It would have been politically unwise for the Conservatives to have opposed the principle of extending the franchise, and so they concentrated their opposition to the exclusion of provisions for redistribution[4] and in some cases to the inclusion of Ireland.[5] The prolonged debate in the Commons[6] and the virtual defeat of the bill in the Lords turned on the issue of redistribution.[7] The Liberals promised a separate bill in the following session but refused to combine the two measures for fear

[1] See No. 1A, p. 130.
[2] See No. 2, p. 131.
[3] See No. 3A, p. 132.
[4] See No. 3B, p. 137.
[5] See No. 3D, p. 142.
[6] See Nos. 3C–G, pp. 138–146.
[7] See No. 3H, p. 147.

that the whole measure would be lost if the Franchise Bill was over-loaded. The Conservatives were afraid that Parliament might be dissolved without a redistribution bill and that a new Parliament, elected on the new franchise with urban working-class voters swamping many of the unredistributed county seats, would pass a much less desirable redistribution measure. Since Lord Salisbury and his colleagues were actually prepared for a more extensive redistribution measure than the Government had contemplated and were not prepared to reject the principle of household suffrage in the counties or to fight the Irish issue to the end, there is no good reason why the settlement finally worked out in the autumn should not have been reached before the first bill was killed by the Lords in July. The explanation lies in the mutual distrust of the two parties and the stubbornness of Salisbury and Gladstone, who were both pretty un-bending until the Queen brought them together. The basic difference between them lay over the role of the House of Lords. Gladstone did not believe that body had the right to dictate to the Government how it should conduct its business, while Salisbury thought it both politi-cally and constitutionally valid for the Conservatives to use their majority in the Lords to do just this. He wanted to force a dissolution, since he thought that in view of the situation in Ireland and Egypt the Conservatives had a good chance of winning an election.

During the summer and early autumn the issue was debated at great length on public platforms throughout the United Kingdom. Several million people were reported to have attended more than one thousand Liberal meetings, while about half a million attended almost two hundred Conservative meetings. Gladstone, to the Queen's indignation,[8] embarked on another Midlothian campaign, making two great speeches in Edinburgh and several in other parts of Scotland. Lord Salisbury, too, was active with hard-hitting speeches in London, Sheffield, Manchester, Glasgow, and other Scottish centers. Joseph Chamberlain, in particular, excited the Queen's indignation by his outspoken attacks on the House of Lords and by his exchange with Lord Salisbury, when they both warned each other of the danger of broken heads.

Several attempts at mediation by moderate peers, often prompt-ed by the Queen, made no impression on the determined nobleman who led the Conservative party. Parliament was summoned for a special autumn session, which opened on 23 October. On reintro-

[8] See No. 4, p. 151.

ducing the Franchise Bill, Gladstone again refused to tie it to redistribution, but he promised to consult the Conservatives regarding the terms of a subsequent redistribution bill. Informal discussions to this end were begun by Lord Hartington with Sir Michael Hicks Beach,[9] but they came to nothing. An exchange between Gladstone and Sir Stafford Northcote was equally unsuccessful.[10] The debate over the Franchise Bill in the Commons was languid and not protracted. The second reading was passed on 7 November by 372 to 232 and the third reading on 11 November without a division.

In the meantime the Queen had made personal appeals to both Gladstone and Salisbury to confer together, but with no immediate results.[11] On 17 November Gladstone and Lord Granville read statements in both houses, undertaking, in return for assurances on the early passage of the Franchise Bill by the Lords, to make known the terms of their Redistribution Bill and to move its second reading in the Commons while the Franchise Bill was in the committee stage in the Lords.[12] On this basis the proposed meeting between the leaders was finally arranged.[13] and, thanks to the preliminary work done by Sir Charles Dilke, the terms of a Redistribution Bill were quickly settled.[14] In this matter Lord Salisbury turned out to be much more radical than the Prime Minister and the bill eventually agreed upon went a good deal further than the original government draft.[15]

As a result of Conservative pressure, the bill abolished all parliamentary boroughs with population under 15,000 (the Government had been content with 10,000); took one member away from all boroughs under 50,000 (compared to 40,000 in the original scheme); and, with a few exceptions, made single-member constituencies the rule.

On the basis of this agreement the Franchise Bill was passed by the House of Lords and became law on 5 December. It added 1,762,000 voters to the electorate. The Redistribution Bill was introduced into

[9] See No. 5A, p. 152. Sir Michael Hicks Beach (1843–1911) was a senior Conservative minister under Disraeli and Salisbury.

[10] See No. 5C, p. 153. Sir Stafford Northcote (1818–1887) was Conservative leader in the House of Commons.

[11] See No. 5B, p. 153.

[12] See No. 5E, p. 156. The Second Earl Granville (1845–1891) was Liberal leader in the House of Lords.

[13] See No. 5F and G, pp. 157 and 158.

[14] See No. 6A and B, pp. 158 and 160. Sir Charles Dilke (1843–1911) was president of the Local Government Board.

[15] See No. 6C, p. 161.

the House of Commons before Christmas, finally passed both Houses, and became law the following spring. It survived the criticisms of the Whigs—who regretted the disappearance of most double-member constituencies, which had enabled them to get elected in the company of Radical partners—and of a few Radicals, who had agitated for some sort of proportional representation.[16]

Historians have had much less to say about the Reform Acts of 1884–1885 than those of 1832 and 1867. Charles Seymour, writing in 1915, saw the act of 1884 as "the culmination of the process begun in 1832,"[17] but he recognized that the Redistribution Act of 1885 left many anomalies, although it went much further than the previous acts towards the principle of representation by population.[18] Dr. McCord sees the passage of the Reform Acts of 1832, 1867, and 1884–1885 as "an excellent example of Britain 'muddling through' to a tolerably satisfactory solution." In his view Britain was transformed into a democracy by the nineteenth-century Reformers without their knowing entirely what they were doing.[19] It is true that much remained to be done, for all adult females and 40 percent of the adult males were still without the vote,[20] but in the early twentieth century this was to be achieved with remarkably little struggle.[21] The Franchise Acts of 1867 and 1884 led inevitably to those of 1918 and 1928; and in the political field they made possible, indeed likely, the formation of a Labour party in 1900.

[16] See No. 6D, p. 163.
[17] See No. 7A, p. 164.
[18] See No. 7B, p. 168.
[19] See No. 7C, p. 169.
[20] See Neal Blewett, "The Franchise in the United Kingdom 1885–1918," *Past and Present*, No. 32 (1965), pp. 28–56.
[21] See below, pp. 173–175.

1   *Radical Pressure for Reform*

(A) VIEWS OF JOSEPH CHAMBERLAIN

Besides this parliamentary work, which was very severe, I undertook in this year a great number of platform engagements and commenced the campaign of constructive Radicalism which soon brought me into conflict with the Whigs—both in the Cabinet and outside. The Radicals in the Cabinet were now only Dilke and myself and found our views ignored or outvoted by the majority of our colleagues. In the country, however, our opinions were endorsed by at least four-fifths of the Liberal Party. It was clear that this state of things could not continue indefinitely and that as soon as the franchise was extended the policy of the Government would have to be modified in the Radical sense. My first effort was to induce the Cabinet to take up the franchise question as early as possible and to separate it from redistribution which was sure to provoke local jealousies and would raise an opposition that might be fatal to the Franchise Bill. I desired also to secure the equality of franchise throughout the Three Kingdoms and to prevent the interposition of any fancy vote such as the cumulative or minority vote, which was then being strongly supported by Courtney, Fawcett, and some other members of the Liberal Party. These were the main objects of the platform campaign of 1883.

(B) DILKE TO CHAMBERLAIN, 30 MARCH 1883

Mr G. called me out last night to his room and talked to me very freely and for a long time. He has never before spoken of next year's County Franchise Bill except with the statement that he would be gone before it—but on this occasion he talked of it with warm interest without saying that, and he left the impression on my mind that his present intention is to stay with us and to conduct next year's bill. Harcourt to-night let me pump his views as to the application of the reform to Ireland. He is strongly with us which is important.

SOURCE. C. H. D. Howard, ed., *Joseph Chamberlain, A Political Memoir* (London: The Batchworth Press, 1953), pp. 86–87. Reprinted by permission of the Hamlyn Publishing Group Limited.

SOURCE. J. L. Garvin, *Life of Joseph Chamberlain* (London: Macmillan & Co. Ltd., 1932), Vol. I, p. 390. Reprinted by permission of the publisher.

2   *The Cabinet Decision on Reform*

GLADSTONE TO QUEEN VICTORIA, 4 JANUARY 1884

Mr. Gladstone submits his humble duty to your Majesty, and humbly reports that the Cabinet met this day to consider some leading points of Parliamentary business for the approaching Session.

They advise that the first great measure of the year should be a Bill for extending to the Counties the occupation franchise, and also the lodger franchise, now enjoyed in Boroughs, and for rendering it uniform as far as may be in town and country, and throughout the Three Kingdoms.

Certain limited franchises of a miscellaneous kind ought, as they conceive, to drop with the present holders: but they propose to leave the whole substance of the property franchises, now subsisting in Counties, unaltered, only making provision against spurious votes by restraining subdivision and rent-charges.

The safe working of the household franchise in Boroughs has removed, in the judgment of your Majesty's advisers, all, even the most shadowy, grounds for apprehension from the enfranchisement of what may be considered as even a safer class of the population.

The reasons formerly urged for combining redistribution of seats with the franchise lose nearly all their force in view of a large though not absolute assimilation; while the reasons against it subsist in still fuller force than heretofore, and the Cabinet conceive the severance of the two measures to be recommended in the highest degree by public reasons.

But they think that the question of redistribution may conveniently be taken up by the present Parliament, in the year following the settlement of the Franchise. And they have sufficiently conversed upon the subject to warrant the belief that upon leading principles there is likely to be found much harmony in their practical views. . . .

SOURCE. G. E. Buckle, ed., *Letters of Queen Victoria*, second series (London: John Murrey Ltd., 1926), Vol. III, pp. 467–468. Reprinted by permission of the publisher.

3 *The Parliamentary Debate on the Franchise Bill of 1884*

(A) GLADSTONE INTRODUCING THE BILL, 28 FEBRUARY

I conceive that this Bill—this proposition—may be presented to the House under any one, and indeed under all, of three distinct and several aspects . . . it is a proposal in satisfaction of a pledge; it is a proposal to meet a desire; but, above all, it is a proposal, in my view, and I think I may say in our view, to add strength to the State. I am not prepared to discuss admission to the franchise as it was discussed 50 years ago, when Lord John Russell had to state, with almost bated breath, that he expected to add in the Three Kingdoms 500,000 to the constituencies. It is not now a question of nicely calculated less or more. I take my stand on the broad principle that the enfranchisement of capable citizens, be they few or by they many—and if they be many so much the better—gives an addition of strength to the State. The strength of the modern State lies in the Representative system. . . . Sir, I may say—it is an illustration which will not occupy more than a moment—that never has this great truth been so vividly illustrated as in the War of the American Republic. The convulsion of that country between 1861 and 1865 was, perhaps, the most frightful which ever assailed a national existence. The efforts which were made on both sides were marked. The exertions by which alone the movement was put down were not only extraordinary, they were what would antecedently have been called impossible; and they were only rendered possible by the fact that they proceeded from a nation where every capable citizen was enfranchised, and had a direct and an energetic interest in the well-being and the unity of the State. Sir, the only question that remains in the general argument is, who are capable citizens? . . .

It is proposed, in the main, to enfranchise the county population on the footing, and according to the measure, that has already been administered to the population of the towns. What are the main constituents of the county population? First of all, they are the minor tradesmen of the country, and the skilled labourers and artizans in all the common arts of life, and especially in connection with our great mining industry. Is there any doubt that these are

SOURCE. *Hansard's Parliamentary Debates*, third series, Vol. 285, cols. 107–109, 114–115, 121–122, 125–129, 131–134.

capable citizens? You hon. Gentlemen opposite have yourselves asserted it by enfranchising them in the towns; and we can only say
that we heartily subscribe to the assertion. But besides the artizans
and the minor tradesmen scattered throughout our rural towns, we
have also to deal with the peasantry of the country. Is there any
doubt that the peasantry of the country are capable citizens, qualified
for enfranchisement, qualified to make good use of their power as
voters? This is a question which has been solved for us by the first
and second Reform Bills; because many of the places which under the
name of towns are now represented in this House are really rural
communities, based upon a peasant constituency. For my part, I
should be quite ready to fight the battle of the peasant upon general
and argumentative grounds. I believe the peasant generally to be, not
in the highest sense, but in a very real sense, a skilled labourer. He
is not a man tied down to one mechanical exercise of his physical
powers. He is a man who must do many things, and many things which
require in him the exercise of active intelligence. . . . If he has a defect,
it is that he is too ready, perhaps, to work with and to accept the
influence of his superiors—superiors, I mean, in worldly station. But
that is the last defect that hon. Gentlemen opposite will be disposed
to plead against him, and it is a defect that we do not feel ourselves
entitled to plead, and that we are not at all inclined to plead. We
are ready to take him as he is, and joyfully bring him within the
reach of this last and highest privilege of the Constitution. . . .

But I now come to the main change of the Bill. It is this. I have
said there were four occupation franchises in boroughs, one of them
the £10 clear yearly value, the other three, the household, the lodger,
and the service franchise.[1] Those three we propose to import into the
counties precisely as they are to be in the boroughs. Now, I hope
that will be clearly understood, because I wish to fasten attention upon
it, as it is the main, the most operative, and the most extensive,
perhaps I should also say the most beneficial, change that is proposed.

Well, then, with regard to the property franchises, I will not dwell
upon them at length, but I will simply for the present say this much—
We maintain the property franchises in principle, but we propose
provisions which we think are necessary, in order to secure them
against abuses which are known in many parts of the country, and
which in some parts are grievous and menacing to the people. Now,

---

[1] A new franchise included in the Bill for certain officers and servants who occupied
houses without paying rent.

I wish to keep together all that relates to the question of occupation. Sir, a fundamental part of the structure of this Bill is the union of the Three Kingdoms in one measure and essentially, so far as we, without undue complexity, can achieve it, not only in one measure, but in one and the same franchise.

Now, let me look at the arguments in favour of separating legislation on the franchise and legislation on redistribution. I have said our measure is incomplete, and that there has never been a complete measure. But our measure is complete in one vital respect, in which no measure heretofore presented to Parliament has been complete. It is absolutely complete as to its area. In our opinion there was an imperative necessity for making it complete as to its area. I, for one, should be no party to the responsibility of bringing in on this occasion three separate Bills. All the three countries have a case for enfranchisement arising out of the insufficiency of the present constituencies as compared with what they might be; but of the three the strongest is that of Ireland. I could bear no part in the responsibility of passing, perhaps, a Reform Bill for England, and, perhaps, a Reform Bill for Scotland, and then leaving a Reform Bill for Ireland to take its chance. I do not wish to rest on my own impression of what would happen. But I have noticed the tone of Conservative organs, and the language of those Conservative organs is, in effect, that there may be something to be said for extending the franchise in England and in Scotland, but to extend it in Ireland is madness. ["Hear, hear!" and laughter.] That is a Conservative organ. That is an indication of what would probably happen, I do not say in this House, but "elsewhere." Under these circumstances, the necessity of a complete measure in point of area is, I would say, absolute, and nothing will induce us to part with the principle. Next, I would ask the House to consider what it is that we ought really to attempt. What has been the effect of uniting redistribution with franchise legislation since 1832? It has been that the redistribution has been of a trivial character, hardly purchasing a postponement of the question, and in reality, and in regard to its broader principles, has simply given the question the go-bye. Some people may be innocent enough to think that our opponents are to be conciliated by uniting redistribution with franchise legislation. We had some experience of that matter in 1866, and we found that, confident and sanguine, and perhaps a little ferocious, as our opponents were before we introduced our Redistribution Bill, when we introduced it their appetites were whetted, became keener than ever, and still more lively was the rush made on every occasion at the unfortunate Bill, until it, and still better the Government which proposed it, were brought to their extinction. In 1867 the number of seats liberated was 38 [sic], and they were liberated by a peculiar process, and by leaving a large number of small towns with one Member. We have to face the question, whether places with 3,000, 4,000 or 5,000 inhabitants are to continue to possess the sole power of returning a Representative to Parliament? The uniting of the two descriptions of legislation has resulted formerly in the inefficient handling of redistribution. If redistribution is to be touched at all, it must be touched more broadly.

What will be the effect of introducing a plan of redistribution? It is quite evident we ought to have some regard to what has happened before. There was one effective plan known to Parliament—the plan of 1831–1832. What was the effect of that plan? The effect was two-fold—in the first place, it multiplied six-fold the labour of the Reform Bill. In Committee on the Reform Bill there were three nights occupied upon the franchise legislation; 24 nights were occupied on redistribution; and the effect of associating redistribution with legislation on the franchise would be to produce at present a result not very different. More than that, the franchise legislation has opponents who find it difficult to show their colours. Redistribution is their favourite study; but it is impossible not to observe this fact—that of the three political crises produced in connection with Reform legislation, every one has been produced by redistribution, and not one by the franchise. . . .

I have the strongest appeal to make to its [the bill's] friends. I entreat them not to endanger the Bill by additions. This Bill is in no danger from direct opposition. It has some danger to encounter from indirect opposition; but of these dangers from indirect opposition, I for one am not afraid, unless they be aggravated by the addition of dangers which it may have to encounter from friendship. For I do not hesitate to say that it is just as possible for friends to destroy the measure by additions which it will not bear, as it is for enemies. If I may presume to tender advice, it is this—Ask yourselves whether the measure is worth having. What does it do, and what does it do in comparison with what has been done before? In 1832 there was passed what was considered a Magna Charta of British liberties; but that Magna Charta of British liberties added, according to the previous estimate of Lord John Russell, 500,000, while according to the results considerably less than 500,000 were added, to the entire constituency of the three countries. After 1832 we come to 1866. At that time the total constituency of the United Kingdom reached 1,364,000. By the

Bills which were passed between 1867 and 1869[2] that number was raised to 2,448,000. And now, Sir, under the action of the present law the constituency has reached in round numbers what I would call 3,000,000. . . . The Bill, if it passes as presented, will add to the English constituency over 1,300,000 persons. It will add to the Scotch consistency, [constituency] Scotland being at present rather better provided for in this respect than either of the other countries, over 200,000, and to the Irish constituency over 400,000; or, in the main, to the present aggregate constituency of the United Kingdom taken at 3,000,000, it will add 2,000,000 more, nearly twice as much as was added since 1867, and more than four times as much as was added in 1832. Surely, I say, that is worth doing, that is worth not endangering. Surely that is worth some sacrifice.

This is a measure with results such as I have ventured to sketch them that ought to bring home to the mind of every man favourable to the extension of popular liberty, the solemn question what course he is to pursue in regard to it. I hope the House will look at it as the Liberal Party in 1831 looked at the Reform Bill of that date, and determined that they would waive criticism of minute details, that they would waive particular preferences and predilections, and would look at the broad scope and general effect of the measure. Do that upon this occasion. It is a Bill worth having; and if it is worth having, again I say it is a Bill worth your not endangering. Let us enter into no bye-ways which would lead us off the path marked out straight before us; let us not wander on the hill-tops of speculation; let us not wander into the morasses and fogs of doubt. We are firm in the faith that enfranchisement is a good, that the people may be trusted—that the voters under the Constitution are the strength of the Constitution. What we want in order to carry this Bill, considering as I fully believe that the very large majority of this country are favourable to its principle—what we want in order to carry it is union and union only. What will endanger it is disunion and disunion only. Let us hold firmly together and success will crown our effort. You will, as much as any former Parliament that has conferred great legislative benefits on the nation, have your reward, and

> "*Read your history in a nation's eyes,*"

for you will have deserved it by the benefits you will have conferred. You will have made this strong nation stronger still; stronger by its

[2]An act amending the compounding provisions of the 1867 act.

closer union without; stronger against its foes, if and when it has any foes without; stronger within by union between class and class, and by arraying all classes and all portions of the community in one solid compacted mass round the ancient Throne which it has loved so well, and round a Constitution now to be more than ever powerful, and more than ever free.

(B) LORD JOHN MANNERS MOVING AN AMENDMENT TO THE SECOND READING, 24 MARCH

If it is thought necessary and wise to increase that representation of the peasantry, nothing could be more easily or more satisfactorily accomplished than by increasing the number of agricultural boroughs. The proposal of Her Majesty's Government, however, is to subvert the existing system, and to substitute for it someting that will totally supersede it. We say, before you subvert the whole system and substitute a new one for it, let us see what your new scheme is in its details and in its entirety. It is, therefore, in no spirit of terror or craven fear— with no unworthy suspicion of our fellow-countrymen, and with no desire to shut our eyes to the shortcomings of our existing representative system, but as prudent guardians of existing institutions, as faithful Representatives of our constituencies, and as loyal upholders of the integrity of the Empire—that we claim full and complete knowledge and information on all these points which I have ventured to bring before the House, and I will conclude by making an appeal to Her Majesty's Government in the words of the ancient Greek warrior—

> *"Remove this cloudy darkness: clear the sky*
> *That we may see our fate, and die at least,*
> *If such thy will, in th' open face of day."*

Sir, I beg leave to move the Amendment standing in my name.

Amendment proposed,

"To leave out from the word 'That' to the end of the Question, in order to add the words 'this House declines to proceed further with a measure, having for its object the addition of two million voters to the electoral body of the United Kingdom, until it has before it the entire scheme contemplated by the Government for the amendment of the Representation of the People,'"

—instead thereof.

SOURCE. *Hansard's Parliamentary Debates*, third series, Vol. 286, cols. 633–634.

(C) JOSEPH CHAMBERLAIN, SECOND READING, 27 MARCH

. . . The objections which have been made are not confined absolutely and strictly to its incompleteness. We have heard again to-night from several Members the old allegation that the country is apathetic, and that there is no pressure on the subject. . . .

Although there have been no riots up to the present time—nothing to satisfy the noble Lord—yet I think there have been ample signs of the opinion of the country and of the interest taken in this question. The last Recess was distinguished above most Recesses by the activity of the debate which went on during its course; and, on the whole, I am afraid I must say that our opponents were more active than we were. They had more time at their disposal, and they were the attacking party. On the whole, they held, I believe, more meetings than we did. I am not going to lay stress upon our meetings. You say they arose from a mere mechanical agitation. Meetings of thousands of representatives from all parts of the country, and meetings equally numerous in localities, are regarded as the creatures of the Caucus; while the meetings of the Constitutional Committees, held in the public-houses, are recognized as the free and full expression of public opinion. They are the free and full expression of the public-house opinion, I have no doubt. But what I want to point out is, that at these meetings, whether held in the open or in public-houses, in not a single instance throughout the whole of the Recess, as far as my memory goes or my knowledge extends, has there been a single case of a solitary resolution having been passed condemning the extension of the franchise. Our meetings, one and all, passed resolutions unanimously, or by vast majorities, in favour of the extension of the franchise. Why have you not accepted the challenge? You say you are certain that the country is with you. Why, then, did you not pass resolutions to that effect at your meetings, and call upon Parliament to discharge this question from its thoughts and give its attention to other business. As far as I know, in not one single case has any resolution hostile to this Bill been passed even at a Conservative meeting. If hon. Gentlemen opposite are really in doubt as to the opinion of the country, it is a doubt which I am inclined to think will be removed before the discussion is finally closed. I do not think we shall be able to gratify the noble Lord the Member for Woodstock (Lord Randolph Churchill).

SOURCE. *Hansard's Parliamentary Debates*, third series, Vol. 286, cols. 952–962.

I do not think we can get up outrages to order, as the right hon. Gentleman the Member for the University of Cambridge (Mr. Raikes) amiably imputes to us. That is not our line. . . .

We are told the time is inopportune. I should like to know when the time would be opportune in the minds of the Tory Party for a measure of Reform. I would undertake to have drafted a Resolution any time in the last 10 years, which would command the united support of the Tory Party, declaring a measure of Reform inopportune at that particular time. This matter was brought before the House on the 13th of May, 1874, by my right hon. Friend the present Chief Secretary to the Lord Lieutenant of Ireland (Mr. Trevelyan). It was opposed, on the ground that it was inopportune, by Mr. Disraeli, who was then the Leader of the House, who stated that its inopportuneness arose from the fact that an attempt had just been made to start a national union of agricultural labourers, and the labourers were in a state of excitement, which was not favourable to the impartial consideration of such a measure. In July, 1875, the matter was again brought before the House of Commons. This time the Trades Union movement of agricultural labourers had settled into a normal condition, and there was no particular excitement. But the measure was still inopportune. It was inopportune, because the House of Commons were told it would delay the great social measures of the Conservative Party. On the 30th of May, 1876, the expression was again used. At that time the country had seen something of the great social measures which the Tory Party had it in their hearts to pass, and that excuse would not pass muster a second time. The Conservative Party was rather hard up for an excuse. They did not declare it inopportune; but they said it was really indecent to bring forward a Motion for a third time which in the same Parliament had been twice condemned by large majorities. I confess it seems to me the time is never inopportune to do a just thing. The difficulty I have is in justifying the delay which has already taken place. . . .

We are told that this Bill, if passed, will annihilate the agricultural interests. Well, that is a most extraordinary statement. When you proposed to enfranchise all the artizans in the towns, I am not aware that the manufacturers said that their interests would be annihilated by the political rights you gave to their workmen. They thought—and thought rightly—that the interests of themselves and their workpeople were identical, and they rejoiced that their workpeople were to be permitted to exercise Constitutional rights. Why, then, is the agricultural interest in a different position? Is it pretended that the interests of the landlords and the interests of the tenant farmers are interests which are hostile to those of the agricultural labourers? That is a very dangerous admission to make. For my part, I say that the greatest of agricultural interests is the interests of the men who till the soil. Those are the interests which we ought to care for, and they are interests which will be advanced by this Bill. They are interests which have been too long neglected and ignored, very much to the injury of the class concerned. What has happened in consequence of the agricultural labourers not having a voice in this House? They have been robbed of their land. [Cries of "No, no!" and "Withdraw!"] I repeat that they have been robbed of their land. ["Prove it!"] They have been robbed of their rights in the commons. ["No, no!"] They have been robbed of their open spaces—["No, no!"]—I do not say intentionally, with any desire on the part of this House or of those who were answerable for those proceedings to injure them, but in ignorance of their interests and rights, for which, unfortunately, they had no spokesman in this House. . . .

In what I am saying now I am not bringing any charge against either Party in this House in regard either to the robbery of the land or the robbery of endowments. I take shame to the Liberal Party quite as much as to the Conservative Party. We are both to blame; but what I argue is, that these wrongs would never have been committed had the agricultural labourers had a voice in this House and been able to speak. Another objection that has been taken has been embodied in an illustration of the noble Lord the Member for North Leicestershire (Lord John Manners), which I think not altogether felicitous. He said that this Bill was a cheque for two millions, drawn payable to the order of the President of the Board of Trade and the Member for the City of Cork (Mr. Parnell). In the first place, I would ask the noble Lord, if this is true, why on earth is it he does not come forward like a man and vote against the second reading of the Bill? . . .

As far as I am concerned, I am flattered by the good opinion the noble Lord expresses of my influence in the country; but his argument comes to this—he refuses to give the franchise to anyone who he is not certain beforehand will support the Tory Party, and, above all, will renounce the President of the Board of Trade and all his works. I think he cannot be serious in what he says in my case. The noble Lord referred to the influence the hon. Member for the City of Cork would obtain. His terror of me is simulated; but I have no doubt he is sincerely afraid of the hon. Member for the City of Cork. He described that hon. Member as likely to become, by this Bill, the Grand

Elector over four-fifths of Ireland. I think that happily describes the present position of the hon. Member. Nobody denies the great influence the hon. Member at present exercises over the constituencies of Ireland; but I am certain that this Bill will make no material change in that great influence. But, in any case, whether it does or not, unless the House is prepared to abandon all idea of a Constitutional treatment of the Irish Question, and all idea of a representative system in Ireland, let us take care that the representative system there shall be a reality and not a sham—not a mere fraud and imposition upon the public. . . .

Let us see what the fact is. In Great Britain, excluding Ireland, one in 10 of the population have votes; in Ireland only one in every 25; there are, therefore, two and a-half times as many electors in proportion in Great Britain as there are in Ireland. The result is that the position of Ireland at the present moment, with regard to the franchise, is worse now than was the position of England and Scotland before the Act of 1867. . . .

Then there is an argument which I almost regret to find used at all in the debate in reference to the Irish vote—it is what I may call the mud-cabin argument. We are told—and I am afraid truly—that half the country population in Ireland live in mud-cabins. That, no doubt, is very deplorable. But I want to ask hon. Gentleman whether that deplorable state of things is likely to be remedied by refusing to give to the inhabitants of the mud-cabins in Ireland an articulate voice to express the misery and wretchedness of their condition? We have heard a good deal lately about the dwellings of the poor in the large towns of England, and I am afraid we have not much to boast of in that respect in comparison with Ireland. I am afraid it has been sufficiently proved that the condition of a great portion of our population, numbering even millions, is such that they live in a state which is repugnant to humanity, and under sanitary conditions which make morality almost impossible; and they are, in this respect, at all events, in a worse position than the inhabitants of the mud-cabins in Ireland, in that our fellow-countrymen, instead of being surrounded by open spaces and living in the free air, live in poisonous courts and stifling dens, from which they cannot escape even into the fresh air. It is to people living in these conditions that the Conservative Party have given votes, and have not scrupled to enfranchise as householders or lodgers. Every one of these people living in the dwellings I now speak of—every one of them—is entitled to claim the vote either as householder or lodger. . . .

I may conclude the remarks which I have ventured to address to the House by pointing out that the issue before the House is really an extremely simple one. We propose to widen the foundations of our political institutions. We propose to associate the largest possible number of capable citizens in the work of government. We are at least as anxious as hon. Gentlemen opposite to proceed, at the earliest possible moment, with the consideration of the next and still more important step of redistributing political power. But we will not consent to jeopardize the success of these great and beneficent reforms by coupling them together, in the vain hope that thereby we may conciliate opponents who are hostile to both. I hope the House of Commons will be true to its pledges and its traditions, and that this Bill will pass with a great majority. Then, perhaps, the House of Lords will be true to its traditions also. In that case let the nation decide between us; and I, for one, have no fear of the result.

(D) SIR MICHAEL HICKS BEACH, SECOND READING, 1 APRIL

... The great difficulty in dealing with Ireland is the fact that the general sympathy is with those individuals who commit crime, because in committing crime they oppose themselves to the Law and Government of the country, and that general sympathy is due to the unfortunate circumstance that a considerable majority of the Irish people are disloyal to the connection between the two Kingdoms. The position is that you are offering political privileges to a people whom you can only govern by the most stringent powers which have ever been conferred on an Irish Government in our time. You are offering this popular franchise to a country where you have frequently to put down political meetings lest they should turn into something like civil war. It seems to me that nothing can be more serious than such a state of affairs. The President of the Board of Trade [Chamberlain] said that a Franchise Bill must be brought in this year, and that Ireland must be included in it; for if it were postponed to 1885 the question of Reform for Ireland would get mixed up with the renewal of the Peace Preservation Acts in that year; and the right hon. Gentleman was sensible of the palpable absurdity of offering a

SOURCE. *Hansard's Parliamentary Debates*, third series, Vol. 286, cols. 1309–1310.

Franchise Bill with one hand and a renewal of the Peace Preservation Acts with the other. Surely the proposals of the Government are not less incongruous when they are compelled to maintain these Acts. Have the Government really pictured to themselves the position in which the passing of the Bill may place them in regard to the Irish representation? Addressing a meeting in the winter, the noble Lord the Secretary of State for War said there were many in this country, who were not confined to the Conservative Party, who would view with considerable dislike and apprehension any measure likely to increase the number or the power of the Irreconcilable Party in Parliament. I listened with great attention to the speech of the noble Lord the other evening, and it occurred to me that the noble Lord was by no means satisfied in his own mind that this would not be the result of the measure before the House. All he said was that the measure, by increasing the size of Irish constituencies, might make them less amenable to the influence of the hon. Member for the City of Cork (Mr. Parnell). If it be so, I am afraid it will only be because the new electors will be disposed to prefer someone more violent and more hostile to England than even that hon. Member, and that surely is not a result which can be looked upon with satisfaction by any Member of the Government. The noble Lord said that the real representation of the loyal minority in Ireland was to be found in the Members from England and Scotland. I am afraid the loyal minority in Ireland would hardly accept that view, and I do not know why they should. . . .

(E) HENRY BROADHURST,[3] SECOND READING, 3 APRIL

. . . It had been frequently alleged in that House that there was no feeling among the mass of people in favour of the extension of the franchise. To that assertion he begged to give a flat contradiction. If the workmen who felt strongly on that question would only address their letters to hon. Members who were opposed to that change instead of to those who supported it, he ventured to say that opinion on the opposite side of the House on that subject would be materially modified. Speaking, as he thought he had a right to do, for the

SOURCE. *Hansard's Parliamentary Debates*, third series, Vol. 286, cols. 1552–1554.

[3] Henry Broadhurst (1840–1911), a stonemason and trade union official, was one of the first working-class members of Parliament.

organized trades of the United Kingdom, he could assure the House that a Motion in favour of the extension of the franchise had been one of the chief Resolutions brought before their annual Congresses ever since the present Government had been in power, and each successive year the Resolution had been stronger. At the Congress of September last, a fear being expressed that the Government might betray the country and not deal with the question in the present Parliament, the Parliamentary Committee of the Congress were instructed to urge the Government by all means in their power to make this the principal subject for the present Session. But that was not all. On the 31st of January a deputation of trades representing the organizations of the United Kingdom waited on the Prime Minister to declare to him their anxiety for a speedy dealing with that subject. That deputation was not an ordinary one. It included about 240 or 250 delegates coming from all parts of the country, whose whole expenses and time were paid for by their union funds and voted by their respective lodgers. He reckoned that its cost to the whole of the trades was not less than £700 or £800—a sum, he need hardly say, which the trade unions of this country would not spend on any matter which they had not deeply at heart. He would now like to say a few words with regard to the Bill itself. In doing so he could not congratulate the Government on the production of a measure which was satisfactory to his mind. It was far too complicated; it had too many qualifications; it was shaped too much to suit the prejudices and the privileges of the rich and the upper classes, rather than shaped to meet the question of the franchise fairly and honestly, as it should be. He saw no reason why any man should be entitled to two votes because he was a freeholder of landed property in the country. That was a mere concession to ancient monopolies, and the privilege should be abolished. His view in regard to this question was that there should be one vote to one man; and the only qualification he should possess was that of being of sufficient age and of capacity to exercise it. By the jugglery of the lodger franchise and by the long residence which was necessary for qualification they effectually deprived thousands of their best citizens of the franchise. . . .

Returning to the question of the agricultural labourers, he much regretted that there was no one of their order there to plead their cause, and give a direct denial to the charge of incapacity and ignorance so constantly brought against them. He contended that the agricultural labourers were as capable of exercising the franchise as many of the farmers themselves.

(F) G. J. GOSCHEN,[4] SECOND READING, 7 APRIL

. . . I find that in 30 county constituencies out of 95 the addition to be made to the constituency from what I may call the industrial and urban element will be so great as to entirely outvote the agricultural constituents. I can refer hon. Members to industrial statistics upon these points, and many hon. Members know these facts from their own experience. The urban element will be strongly increased; and it must be so, because the boroughs will be left unchanged by this Bill, and although there are service and other franchises, they are exceedingly slight and insignificant compared with the numbers which will be otherwise introduced. Hon. Members will see that this process will go on; that a large number of urban voters residing in unrepresented towns or the suburbs of boroughs will be placed in the counties in numbers entirely out of proportion to the labourers, the landlords, and others. When I say that, I refer not only to the dwellers in towns, but to all who have affinities, political and otherwise, with what I may call the urban democracy. It is the industrial and the urban, the gregarious classes, which will be enfranchised in large numbers; and it is the wish of hon. Members that they should be enfranchised in those large numbers. They will be enfranchised in such numbers that in 30 county constituencies returning 60 Members there will be an entire transfer of political power from an agricultural and farm class to the urban class. I have looked carefully into the matter; and it is not a question between the Conservative and the Liberal side. I hope the House will see that I have not dwelt upon any Party consideration; but it is a question between the rural and the urban element. I say, with reference to the next Parliament, to which we refer redistribution and the protection of minorities, we shall find that it will be reinforced by 60 Members returned for county constituencies, which will have become practically urban or industrial. But I will only assume 40 votes. We know there will be a gain to the hon. Member for the City of Cork (Mr. Parnell) of, at least, 10 or 15 votes; and the result will be that in this new Parliament there will be at least 50 Members, representing 100 on a Division, who will strengthen the urban Democracy, and who will have in their hands power for the purpose of the Redistribution Bill, and for the resisting of those securities for which some of us have pressed so much.

SOURCE. *Hansard's Parliamentary Debates*, third series, Vol. 286, cols. 1878–1880.

[4] G. J. Goschen (1831–1907), a former Liberal minister, became Conservative Chancellor of the Exchequer in 1886.

I have endeavoured to persuade myself that I could vote for this Bill; but I have not been able to persuade myself. My Party seem to breathe an atmosphere of Utopia, and to feel a confidence I cannot share. But I wish this House to feel assured that if I cannot join hon. Members who will crowd through the Lobbies to carry the second reading of this Bill, that if I must sit silent while the cheers are heard which will greet the victory when the numbers are announced from the Chair, I shall none the less breathe a most fervent and earnest hope that my own misgivings, which compel my dissent, may be put to the rout by the future course of events; and that the Democracy to which the large majority of the House is content to confide the future destinies of this country may stand out in splendid contrast to the Democracy of other countries, and that by its superior fairness and greater moderation it may prove that history does not always repeat itself, and that examples do not always teach a lesson. It is with feelings such as these that I am obliged most reluctantly to announce my intention of voting against this Bill.

(G) PASSAGE OF THE SECOND READING—GLADSTONE TO QUEEN VICTORIA, 7/8 APRIL

Mr. Gladstone offers his humble duty to your Majesty, and humbly reports that he returned to London to-day to attend the debate on the amendment of Lord John Manners, moved against the second reading of the Franchise Bill. Being advised by Sir A. Clark to speak at an early hour of the evening, he rose at about half-past six, and made it his main endeavour to show that the Franchise Bill had been framed in all particulars for the promotion of national objects, and not of the narrower objects of the Liberal Party. . . .

Sir Stafford Northcote rose at a little before midnight. His speech. . . contended that the indications given by the Government as to a scheme of redistribution were at once insufficient, shifting, and alarming, and that the House was therefore not in a condition to proceed with the consideration of the Franchise Bill. . . .

The House divided at half-past one, when the numbers were:

For the second reading	340
For the amendment	210
Majority	130

SOURCE. G. E. Buckle, ed., *Letters of Queen Victoria*, second series (London: John Murray Ltd., 1926) Vol. III, pp. 493–494. Reprinted by permission of the publisher.

The friends of Mr. Parnell on this occasion, for only the second time during this Parliament (in cardinal divisions), voted with the Government.

(H) LORD SALISBURY, HOUSE OF LORDS
SECOND READING, 8 JULY

. . . I am in a condition to know what are the opinions of Conservatives, not only within these walls, but in various parts of the country; and there has never been any adverse feeling to the extension of the suffrage on the ground of the presumed incapacity or unfitness of those to whom it has to be extended. Such a feeling has not been avowed—has not been felt by the Conservative Party in this House or out of it. But the issue turns on a totally different question. The question is—How is political power to be so distributed that all classes may receive their due position in the State, that all interest may be respected, that a true mirror of the actual numerical condition of opinions in this country may be produced within the walls of the other House of Parliament, in order that minorities may be able to receive that just power of expressing their opinions, which is essential to the just protection of their interests, and which belongs, as one of its characteristics, to the first idea of true and genuine representation? We must not for a moment forget—although this debate may almost have banished the fact from our minds—that we are asked to assent to a measure which is absolutely unprecedented in the history of this country. Never before has any Government attempted—certainly, never before, at all events, has any Government succeeded in dealing—with the question of the extension of the franchise without dealing at the same time with the question of redistribution; and never before have we been asked to admit a number of new voters within the pale of the Constitution without provision being made for redistribution of the power so conferred upon them. . . .

The hour is far too late for me to attempt to enter into details; but the fact remains that, from the first creation of our Parliamentary system, there has been a broad and strong distinction between counties and boroughs, and between the rural and the urban parts of the country. We may not always be able to define that distinction with precision, and we may not be able always to say where the one begins

SOURCE. *Hansard's Parliamentary Debates*, third series, Vol. 290, cols 456–460, 463–465, 467–469.

and the other ends—that is, the character of natural as contrasted with
artificial distinctions. But the distinction between them is real, and is
bound up with our everyday life in town and country, and has existed
in our Constitution from the first. This Bill deals with those constituencies which have up to this moment been rural constituencies,
and it projects into them a vast mass of purely urban electors; and the
result of that projection will be that, in a very considerable number of
cases, the balance of power will remain, not with the rural, but with
the urban electors; and that upon all points on which the interests of
the one class are opposed to those of the other the effect of the Bill will
be to efface the opinion of the rural portions of the counties and to
prevent them from having due representation. Do not say that this is
done in justice to the interests of the urban portions of the country,
for they have representation already very largely—even more largely,
more abundantly and superfluously, than any numerical theory as to
their mere numbers of electors can justify. Therefore, you are going
not only to leave them what they have, but to give them this additional
representation at the expense of, and to the destruction of, the rural
element. Another result of your action will be this—there has always
been great difficulty in highly developed representative systems, in
which democratic theories have a large preponderance, to secure the
adequate representation of minorities. In the old times there was no
such difficulty, for there were always a great variety of interests represented; and the result was that the minorities always found themselves
adequately represented. But this Bill altogether overlooks the representation of minorities, and the further you go in the direction of a
dead and mechanical uniformity, the more you expose minorities
to the danger of having their opinions altogether overlooked. That
is what you are doing by this Bill. In these constituencies into which
you propose to project a large mass of urban voters, you have
minorities which find considerable representation. By minorities I do
not mean the rich, or the landowners merely, but the middle classes. . . .
No doubt, your Lordships have heard and studied the very interesting
speech made by my noble Friend the noble Marquess (the Marquess
of Waterford), who so often represents the affairs of Ireland in this
House with such ability. He pointed out that the effects which here
will be anomalous and injurious, in Ireland would be fatal to the
existence of a great class, and that a class upon which the supremacy
of England and the integrity of the Empire largely depends. He
showed, if I remember his figures right, that, whereas there is a loyal
minority of something like 1,500,000, if this Bill passes as it is now,

95 or 96 per cent of the representation of Ireland will pass into hands to which the epithet loyal cannot be applied. My Lords, it is a commonplace of discussion on these questions to tell us that our prophecies in the past were gloomy, and that they have not been fulfilled. In reference to England, that may seem, in some measure, true. If it is true, it is a very great and happy tribute to the qualities of our countrymen. But in respect to Ireland, it is, unfortunately, not true. In this House we warned you 10 years ago of what would be the result of giving the ballot to Ireland. We warned you, and we did the best to carry our warning into effect, that the passing of that measure would take power out of the hands of those who love the English connection and put it in the hands of those who did not love it. Have we been right, or have we been wrong? Has not the result amply justified the very gloomiest warnings that we uttered 10 years ago? The same warning that we uttered then we now utter to you again. This measure in its present incomplete and incohate form, has, among other things, this disadvantage—that it seriously menaces the integrity of the Empire. . . .

Everyone acquainted with the present condition of Parties in the House of Commons knows the power that has been obtained by a particular section connected with the neighbouring Isle, as well as the general course of Business and habits of the House, makes it certain no Government, not even the most powerful, can insure, as a matter of absolute certainty, that a Redistribution Bill should be passed before the Dissolution. But even if it were passed, should we be any better? My Lords, what we want is, not only a Redistribution Bill, but a Redistribution Bill that we can handle; something which, if manifestly unjust, we should be able to modify. But how should we be able to modify it, if we had this pistol put to our heads—"Unless you pass this Bill, you shall have no Bill at all; and you go to the country with a new enfranchisement on the old constituencies?" We shall have no power over such a Bill; and, therefore, not even if they were able absolutely to promise, they could not, if they once allowed this measure to pass out of their and our hands, engage to us that we should have a free hand in modifying the details of redistribution. But, my Lords, when we are told that terrible evils are to result from the course of events, we are tempted to ask whose fault is it? If all those horrible things are to come in consequence of this Bill not passing, why does not some Member of the Government get up and say—"We will put you a clause into the Bill which shall prevent this measure coming into operation until the Redistribution Bill is passed?" If they did that, then the difficulty would be at an end; and if they refuse to do that, on them, and not on us, the responsibility of any consequences will rest. . . .

The noble Earl the Secretary of State for the Colonies made the observation that we were coming into an obvious collision between this House and the vast majority of the people of England. Now, he seemed to have an impression, while dwelling upon that subject, that he was a little open to the charge that he himself was menacing the House of Lords, and, in order to clear himself of that imputation, he said—"I am no more uttering a menace than a man who sees a heavy rain storm before him and calls your attention to the fact." I do not think that gave an accurate simile. I should say that he was more like a man who had previously placed a row of small boys with stones in their hands, some distance off, at a particular spot in the road, and then proceeded to warn you, in a spirit of friendship, that if you went down the road you would probably have stones thrown at you. That is, perhaps, a more exact description of the position of the noble Earl. There are a number of very dirty boys, and some very learned dirty boys, who are employed—I will not say by noble Lords themselves, but at all events employed by the subordinates of noble Lords opposite—for the purpose of vilifying this House and agitating against it; and that is the real answer to all these stories that we shall be misunderstood. . . .

My Lords, we have heard and are told much about the dangers this House is running. I heard, with the greatest pleasure, the speech of the noble Duke opposite (the Duke of Argyll) with respect to the position of this House. We have, as he says, great privileges, and those privileges are balanced by large disabilities; but whatever may be the outcome and balance of those two considerations, which undoubtedly weigh with many, I feel sure that, upon the view of our privileges as presented to us by noble Lords opposite, nobody, no man who values his manhood and his self-respect, and no man who prizes his intellectual freedom, would wish to retain the privileges of the House upon the terms upon which they offer them to us. Just consider what the position is in regard to which all these grandiloquent threats are hurled at our heads. We have to deal with a proposal absolutely unprecedented—a proposal which affects the whole future of the legislation of this country. It threatens to efface some of the most important classes of the country, whose voices, as expressed by their Representatives, have hitherto been heard at Westminster, and it threatens to crush minorities; and it is here, for the first time, we ask to know the whole plan; and we ask, if we may not know the whole plan, at least that such delay may be granted that the people may be consulted upon the question, and the results of this vast change. We are told that even this humble and moderate exercise of independence is sufficient to call down destruction on our heads. I do not believe a word of it; but if it were true, I should say that the powers entrusted to this House were fettered by conditions so humiliating that no man of honour could accept them. I will not, at this hour, detain your Lordships further, though the subject is endless. I will only say this—that the arguments which are addressed to us having reference to existing agitations, or to impending processions and demonstrations, seem to me to be the idlest of all. We know perfectly that demonstrations and expressions of anger can be produced to order by our adversaries so long as the balance at their bankers remains unexhausted. We are taking the course which is the true safeguard of the liberties of the people, and of the institutions of the country, in the presence of vast proposals wholly unprecedented, in the presence of a proposal for a change which is admitted to be so tremendous, that it exceeds the effects of the Revolution of 1688. In the presence of such vast proposals we appeal to the people. We have no fear of the humiliation with which we are threatened. We do not shrink from bowing to the opinion of the people, whatever that opinion may be. If it is their judgement that there should be enfranchisement without redistribution, I should be very much surprised; but I should not attempt to dispute their decision. But now that the people have in no real sense been consulted, when they had, at the last General Election, no notion of what was coming upon them, I feel that we are bound, as guardians of their interests, to call upon the Government to appeal to the people, and by the result of that appeal we will abide.

4   *Royal Criticism of Gladstone's Speeches*

QUEEN VICTORIA TO SIR HENRY PONSONBY,
16 SEPTEMBER 1884

. . . Sir Henry must write somewhat strongly to Mr. Gladstone. He makes great shows of alarm and anxiety, but goes on agitating by his *constant* speeches at every station, without which the country *would not* be *excited*.

SOURCE. G. E. Buckle, ed., *Letters of Queen Victoria*, second series (London: John Murray Ltd., 1926) Vol. III, p. 539. Reprinted by permission of the publisher.

He must be quiet now, and he *must* be *ready also* to meet any proposal in a conciliatory spirit. But this she fears is not in him.

The Queen is *utterly* disgusted with his *stump* oratory—so unworthy of his position—almost under her very nose.[1]

5   *The Solution of the Constitutional Crisis of 1884*

(A) GLADSTONE TO QUEEN VICTORIA, 31 OCTOBER, RE THE HARTINGTON-HICKS-BEACH MEETING

Mr. Gladstone offers his humble duty to your Majesty, and reports that he this day made known to his colleagues in Cabinet the suggestion for a possible settlement of the question of Parliamentary Representation, which he had the honour to receive yesterday through Sir H. Ponsonby. His colleagues agree with him in the opinion that the offer to concede the second reading of the Franchise Bill alone would make no substantial difference in the situation, and they do not see in the suggestion any hopeful means for an adjustment.

Mr. Trevelyan reported to the Cabinet your Majesty's gracious assurance to him of an unwearied anxiety for the settlement of this great question, which the Cabinet received most gratefully, and your Majesty's indisposition to a dissolution of Parliament under the present circumstances, which they conceive to be prompted by a spirit of wisdom.

Mr. Gladstone mentioned a variety of indications from different quarters all tending to show that there is probably a growing anxiety among those of the Opposition for some accommodation: and Lord Hartington mentioned an interview which, with Mr. Gladstone's concurrence, he had held with Sir Michael H. Beach. At that interview, which was of the most confidential character, and entirely without prejudice, Sir M. Beach stated with perfect frankness and fulness his views of Redistribution, which he was understood to share with other leading men of his party, but who or how many they were did not clearly appear. He gave the outline of a very large plan, involving more

---

[1] "Even at Ballater," which is within a few miles of Balmoral, wrote the Queen next day in her Journal; "I think it very unbecoming for the Prime Minister."

SOURCE. G. E. Buckle, ed., *Letters of Queen Victoria,* second series (London: John Murray Ltd., 1926) Vol. III, pp. 564–565. Reprinted by permission of the publisher.

extensive changes than Mr. Gladstone would have thought necessary or desirable. At the same time he is sensible of the vast importance of a settlement, and he believes and hopes that his colleagues will keep their minds open to what may be the exigencies of the time, without any unduly strict prepossessions as to particulars. In this he feels rather confident of your Majesty's approval. . . .

(B) ROYAL INTERVENTION—QUEEN VICTORIA TO LORD SALISBURY, 31 OCTOBER

Though the Queen has already had several indirect communications with Lord Salisbury, she thinks the present crisis of such national and vital importance and the danger to the Constitution, likely to result from a prolonged difference between the two Houses of Parliament, so serious that she writes to him direct.

Considering that the matters now in dispute seem to be capable of adjustment, she hopes that Lord Salisbury will consent that a personal conference between the leaders of the two Parties in both Houses shall take place.

The object of such a meeting would be the exchange of views as to the assurances to be given of the character of the Redistribution Bill. It seems most desirable to the Queen that the questions to be brought before the House should be settled by this Parliament and that without delay some understanding be arrived at.

The Queen feels assured that Lord Salisbury, who has always shown such readiness to meet her wishes, will not object to a meeting which the Queen will gladly facilitate and which she is most anxious to bring about.[1]

(C) GLADSTONE TO QUEEN VICTORIA, 14 NOVEMBER

Mr. Gladstone transmits to your Majesty with his humble duty, and with very deep regret, the enclosed copies of documents dated yesterday and to-day.

[1]The Queen addressed a similar letter to Gladstone.

SOURCE. G. E. Buckle, ed., *Letters of Queen Victoria*, second series (London: John Murray Ltd., 1926) Vol. III, pp. 563–564. Reprinted by permission of the publisher.

SOURCE. G. E. Buckle, ed., *Letters of Queen Victoria*, second series (London: John Murray Ltd., 1926) Vol. III, pp. 571–572. Reprinted by permission of the publisher.

ENCLOSURES

No. 1.

Copy of Query placed in the hands of Sir S. Northcote by Mr. Gladstone at a private conversation on the night of 13th Nov. 1884, which he proposed to communicate to Lord Salisbury.

What assurances will you require about the character of our Redistribution Bill, as a condition of engaging that, if we produce it before the Franchise Bill reaches the Committee in the Lords, and make it a vital question, the Franchise Bill shall then be put forward without difficulty or delay?

No. 2.

Reply of Sir Stafford Northcote

[*Copy.*]   14*th November* 1884

My Dear Mr. Gladstone, The only answer I can give to your question is—that the House of Lords will not part with control over the Franchise Bill till it has the Redistribution Bill before it. But it would be perfectly possible to offer guarantees against any apprehended maltreatment of the Redistribution Bill if the result of previous communications be satisfactory. I remain, yours very faithfully, Stafford H. Northcote.

No. 3.   *Mr. Gladstone to Sir S. Northcote*

[*Copy.*]   *Secret.*   14*th November* 1884.

My Dear Northcote, I understand your note as written on behalf, at least, of Lord Salisbury and yourself.

While thanking you for the conversation of last night, I regret that your reply to my enquiry declines communications which should have for their "objective point" the passing of the Franchise Bill without delay, and substitutes a new basis according to which the Lords would not pass the Franchise Bill until the Seats Bill was before them.

It is not in my power to enter into any negotiation or interchange of views, except to secure the passing of the Franchise Bill without delay. If that were secured I know not of any other demand, likely to be made, which need meet with refusal.

This being so, and there being no material for our further communications, I shall observe strictly the secrecy of our conversation: only desiring to make known to the Queen (not the Cabinet) my query, your reply, and this note in answer.

Of course it is open to me to consider whether, without any allusion to what has passed between us, I shall state publicly on behalf of the

Government the basis on which we are prepared to proceed. I remain, sincerely yours, W. E. Gladstone.

(D) GLADSTONE TO QUEEN VICTORIA, 15 NOVEMBER

Mr. Gladstone reports to your Majesty, with his humble duty, that he this day stated to the Cabinet, not the contents of the documents he had yesterday the honour of forwarding to your Majesty, nor the name of any person in connection with them, but the conclusion which they conveyed to his mind that, so far as leaders of the Tory Party were concerned, the door was now closed against accommodation with the House of Lords.

He ought perhaps to observe in passing that, after obtaining a distinct declaration from Sir Stafford Northcote on his own behalf and that of Lord Salisbury, he felt himself precluded by honour from attempting to establish any separate communication with their immediate friends.

This being so, the question remained whether there should be a public declaration by Lord Granville in the House of Lords, and by Mr. Gladstone in the House of Commons, setting forth the basis upon which your Majesty's advisers are prepared to proceed with respect to the two measures.

The Cabinet approved of this plan, and agreed upon the accompanying paper which, apart from any prefatory or accompanying remark, they think should be delivered textually in both Houses of Parliament on Monday. Some intimation that it is to be made will probably appear in the morning journals of that day, but the subject matter will remain secret until the appointed time.

Your Majesty's Ministers are not without the hope that their declaration may produce an effect upon Peers of moderate opinions as well as in a wider circle. . . .

ENCLOSURE
Declaration to be made in both Houses

Secret

15*th Nov.* 1884. Our object is to secure the passing of the Franchise Bill without delay.

SOURCE. G. E. Buckle, ed., *Letters of Queen Victoria*, second series (London: John Murray Ltd., 1926) Vol. III, pp. 572–574. Reprinted by permission of the publisher.

We could enter into no understanding, and we could take no steps, as to the immediate introduction or prosecution of a Seats Bill, or as to any other particular relating thereto, which did not afford us adequate assurance that we should thereby secure our main object— the passing of the Franchise Bill without delay; that is to say, during the present autumnal sittings.

If we are adequately assured as to the attainment of that object, I am not aware of any demand likely to be made, in relation to proceeding upon the other measure, to which we should not be able to accede.

In illustration of this remark, I may specify the following points.

(1) We should be ready to make the main provisions of the Seats Bill or even the Draft Bill a subject of friendly communication at once and before introduction, and to make every reasonable effort for accommodation; or

To present a Bill conceived in the spirit of the sketch in the House of Commons which Sir S. Northcote, on Friday the 7th November, appeared to receive with satisfaction.

(2) To prosecute the measure with all speed, even to the point of moving the 2nd Reading simultaneously with passing the Franchise Bill into Committee in the House of Lords, or, if that be impracticable, then with any subsequent stage.

(3) To make the passing of the Bill in a form agreeable to the House a vital question, and to use our best efforts to bring it to issue in the House of Commons early in the coming year.

I have been authorised by my colleagues in this matter of such deep interest, to make this public declaration at the present critical moment.

(E) EARL GRANVILLE TO QUEEN VICTORIA, 17 NOVEMBER

Lord Granville presents his humble duty to your Majesty. His statement on the Reform Bills was well received by the House.[2] The relief seemed great on both sides and on the Cross benches. Several Conservative Peers hinted privately their satisfaction.

SOURCE. G. E. Buckle, ed., *Letters of Queen Victoria*, second series (London: John Murray Ltd., 1926) Vol. III, p. 576.

[2]The similar statement in the House of Commons, Mr. Gladstone reported to the Queen, "was received with intense attention, and, so far as could be seen within a short time after, it produced a not inconsiderable effect."

The Duke of Richmond called on me, alluded to your Majesty's wish that the leaders should meet, and pressed that an agreement should be come to for a confidential meeting without prejudice between four Conservative and four Liberal leaders. Lord Granville told him that he was much pleased with the language which the Duke used, and that he thought the statements about to be made to Parliament would greatly facilitate such agreements.

Lord Salisbury asked Lord Granville to give him in writing what he had said in the House. He had asked two questions as to details, which were answered by Lord Granville and the Lord Chancellor.

If Lord Granville may venture to say so, your Majesty must feel rather proud[3] of the powerful influence which your Majesty has brought to bear upon the probable settlement of this burning question. . . .

[*Telegram.*]

18*th Nov.* 1884.—Humble duty.

Lord Salisbury made a conciliatory speech. He said that explanations from Mr. Gladstone subsequent to the first declaration last night induced him to consent. He asked further questions as to your Majesty's Government making the passing a Bill a vital question, and announced that he should propose the adjournment of the Committee for a fortnight. He told Lord Granville that he and Sir Stafford Northcote would be at Mr. Gladstone's and Lord Granville's orders.

(F) THE DUKE OF ARGYLL TO QUEEN VICTORIA, 18 NOVEMBER

Madam, I cannot help writing a line to congratulate your Majesty most heartily upon the acceptance of the compromise offered by Mr. Gladstone. I have no doubt that this has been due to your Majesty's unremitting care for the public interests in the exercise of the influence of the Crown upon all parties.

It is a MOST fortunate conclusion to a most disagreeable and dangerous agitation. The relief expressed in the House to-night was remarkable. I am, your Majesty's faithful and affectionate Subject and Servant, Argyll.

SOURCE. G. E. Buckle, ed., *Letters of Queen Victoria,* second series (London: John Murray Ltd., 1926) Vol. III, p. 577. Reprinted by permission of the publisher.

[3] "Which I certainly am," comments the Queen in her Journal on the 18th November, "or, rather, more than thankful that I have been able to effect this."

(G) SALISBURY'S REASONS FOR NEGOTIATION—SALISBURY
TO CRANBROOK, 18 NOVEMBER

On the whole, we came to the conclusion that we could not safely refuse to enter upon the communications to which the Government invite us. We pledge ourselves to nothing until the result of them is ascertained. If we had taken the other course we should have gone to a dissolution very heavily weighted.

The Carlton meeting was practically unanimous (Redesdale and Oranmore were partly dissentient), and a great many indications combined to prove that the ice was cracking all round us, and that we should have led the party to great disaster if we had declined to negotiate.

6   *The Final Settlement*

(A) EXTRACTS FROM THE QUEEN'S JOURNAL

Windsor Castle, 24th Nov. 1884.   Saw the Duke of Richmond, who, with the Duchess, has come here for one night. He is delighted at the difficulties having been surmounted, but said he had found them very great when he came to Town on the 17th. Lord Cairns had written very strongly to Lord Salisbury, who had called a meeting of a few Peers, which the Duke thought very injudicious, and he felt it his duty to say he considered the state of affairs very serious, and could not be a party to throwing out the Franchise Bill. An arrangement ought now to be come to about the Redistribution Bill. Lord Salisbury was very much annoyed and called a meeting of the whole party, at which it was soon seen that the feeling was in favour of an arrangement. The Duke of Richmond, as well as Lord Cairns, stated again what they had said the day before, to which Lord Salisbury replied he was much grieved to hear it, but gave way, and the Duke hears now, that he after all considers it was much the best course to pursue. The

SOURCE. Lady Gwendolyn Cecil, *Life of Robert Marquis of Salisbury* (London: Hodder and Stoughton Ltd., 1921–1932), Vol. III, p. 121. Reprinted by permission of Collins-Knowlton-Wing, Inc.

SOURCE. G. E. Buckle, ed., *Letters of Queen Victoria*, second series (London: John Murray Ltd., 1926) Vol. III, pp. 582–584. Reprinted by permission of the publisher.

Duke expressed his warm thanks to me for having by my influence brought this to pass.

25th Nov. ... Saw Mr. Gladstone, who is much pleased at the success of the agreement, and at the meetings. He said nothing could have been more pleasant or able than Lord Salisbury and Sir S. Northcote. He could not tell what had brought about the change, and I said I thought it was entirely due to the strong language used by the Duke of Richmond and Lord Cairns, which Mr. Gladstone considers very wise. He spoke of the different plans, and of the Reform of the Franchise Bill. The Opposition were very strong on the minority being sufficiently represented. He considers their plan to be a much greater change than what he had proposed, but thinks the arrangement of Seats according to Seats [? population] is on the whole the best. ...

27th Nov. Mr. Gladstone telegraphed that all points of importance were settled. Saw Lord Salisbury, who seemed less elated, and when I said I hoped all was now well and satisfactorily settled, he replied that there was a most serious hitch. It was about the University votes, which the Government seemed to be inclined to abandon, and which were vital to the Conservatives. He had written in strong terms to Mr. Gladstone, urging him to maintain this, and he hoped it might all come right. Lord Salisbury seemed rather depressed and evidently not exactly pleased at the peaceable arrangement. I said it was a great thing, and he answered, "I think we could have made a good fight," to which I replied, "But at what a price!" He seemed then to agree; spoke in very warm terms of Mr. Gladstone, Lord Granville, and Sir C. Dilke, saying they had been very conciliatory and pleasant to deal with. I said Mr. Gladstone considered Lord Salisbury's plan as far more Radical than his Bill would have been. Telegraphed to Mr. Gladstone saying I heard from Lord Salisbury that a serious difficulty had arisen about the University vote, and I earnestly hoped this would not militate against a final settlement. In the meantime, and before seeing Lord Salisbury, I received a most satisfactory letter from Mr. Gladstone saying that "the delicate and novel communications have been brought to a happy conclusion," thanks me "for the wise, gracious, and steady exercise of influence," and that his "cordial acknowledgments are due to Lord Salisbury and Sir S. Northcote."

(B) AN ACCOUNT BY SIR CHARLES DILKE

[Sir Charles Dilke, president of the Local Government Board and a
Radical member of the Cabinet, was the author of the Government's re-
distribution plan. He had already had several private meetings with Lord
Salisbury.]

"On the 26th, at four o'clock, we met at Downing Street, all five
being present. . . . Lord Salisbury, yielding to my reasoning, gave
up grouping," on the understanding that the Boundary Commissioners were "to keep the urban patches as far as possible by themselves. . . . Ultimately it was settled that single-member districts should
be universal in counties, and that we should leave open for the present
the question of how far it should be applied to boroughs."

" . . . On the next morning, November 27th, Mr. Gladstone, Lord
Granville, Hartington, I, and Chamberlain met before the Cabinet
at 11 o'clock, and kept the Cabinet waiting, the Cabinet having been
called for twelve, and Redistribution alone being considered at it.
I announced at the Cabinet that the Tories proposed and we accepted
single-member districts universally in counties, boundaries to be
drawn by a commission who were to separate urban from rural as
far as possible, without grouping and without creating constituencies
of utterly eccentric shape. The names of the commissioners had been
settled, and both sides were pledged to accept their proposals, unless
the two sides agreed to differ from them.[1]

"The Tories proposed single-member districts almost everywhere in boroughs, and only positively named one exception—the
City of London—but were evidently prepared to make some exceptions. They made our agreement on this point the condition of passing
the Franchise Bill, of giving up the decrease of the Irish members
from 103 to 100 which they urged, of giving up all forms of minority
vote, and of giving up grouping. My own opinion and that of the
Prime Minister were in favour of agreement. Hartington, who much
disliked what he thought would be the extinction of the Whigs by an
omnipresent caucus for candidates' selection, was hostile to the
single-member system. I pointed out that we already proposed in

SOURCE. S. Gwynn and G. M. Tuckwell, *Life of Sir Charles Dilke* (London, 1917), Vol.
II, pp. 75–78.

[1]At the meeting of the 26th "it was agreed that the Boundary Commissioners should
consist of those gentlemen who had been advising me."

our amended scheme 120 single-member borough seats out of 284 borough seats. We had thrown out to the Tories a question as to whether they would accept, say, 184 single-borough seats, and give us, say, not more than 100 for double-member seats; or, if they liked, two-thirds and one-third; and they did not positively decline this suggestion. Mr. Gladstone proposed to "save from compulsory division those urban constituencies, not Metropolitan, which, now possessing dual representation, are to have their representation neither increased nor diminished." (This was the ultimate agreement.) Also, that "cities and towns which are to receive four members and upwards, ten in number, should have one central or principal area set apart with two members." (This was purely personal on Mr. Gladstone's part and was universally rejected.)

"I argued warmly in favour of supporting Lord Salisbury's scheme (upon which he and I were absolutely agreed), I being delighted at having got seven more members for the Metropolis than were given by my scheme in its last form after the Cabinet had cut it down. In order to secure Chamberlain's support I told him "I might be able to save a seat for you and give the extended Birmingham seven if you liked to make that a condition, but in that case I must get one some where for Glasgow also out of the rest of Scotland, which is skinning flints."

"The reception of our proposals by the Cabinet, to which Grosvenor" (the Chief Whip) "had been called in, was not altogether favourable. Childers talked about resigning, and Grosvenor was most hostile. We had the enormous advantage, however, that Chamberlain and I and Mr. Gladstone were the only three people who understood the subject, so that the others were unable to fight except in the form known as swearing at large. I was sent off from the Cabinet to Lord Salisbury to tell him that we could agree. At three o'clock we had a further conference with the Conservative leaders, and came to an agreement on my base, Chamberlain, who was somewhat hostile, yielding to me, I going in and out to him, for he was at Downing Street in another room."

(C) A COMPARISON OF THE ORIGINAL SCHEME WITH THE FINAL ONE

... The two schemes would thus show the following contrasts:

SOURCE. *Annual Register 1884*, p. 254.

DISFRANCHISED

The original Liberal scheme

	LIB.	CON.	H.R.
72 boroughs under 10,000 pop.	30	34	8
6 agricultural boroughs (2 each)	8	4	—
Macclesfield and Sandwich (2 each)	2	2	—

The Gladstone-Salisbury scheme

	LIB.	CON.	H.R.
72 boroughs under 10,000 pop.	30	34	8
19 boroughs between 10,000 and 15,000	10	6	3
6 agricultural boroughs (2 each)	8	4	—
Macclesfield and Sandwich	2	2	—
8 boroughs (2 each)	10	6	—

PARTIALLY DISFRANCHISED

	LIB.	CON.	H.R.
40 boroughs between 10,000 and 40,000	27	11	2
2 counties (Rutland and Hereford)	—	2	—
27 boroughs between 15,000 and 40,000	17	8	2
8 boroughs between 40,000 and 50,000	$5\frac{1}{2}$	$1\frac{1}{2}$	1
2 counties	—	2	—
London City	—	2	—

The combined effect of Schedules A and B would be to extinguish 160 seats, and the 6 seats which had been extinguished for some years would be revived. Of the seats thus made available the counties would get 96, of which 64 were in England; and in addition to existing boroughs new boroughs would be created out of counties which would receive 8 seats. As to the distribution of these, Mr. Gladstone explained that seven would be added to the metropolis, taken partly out of the home counties, and that the total augmentation of metropolitan members would be 37, but the City would lose 2 members. Liverpool would have 6 additional members, Glasgow 4, Birmingham 4, Manchester 3, Leeds 2, and Sheffield 3. As to the counties, Yorkshire would have 16 additional members, Lancashire 15, Middlesex 5, Cork 5, Durham 4, and Lanarkshire 4. With regard to the rest, he said the Government had decided to apply to all the electoral areas of the country regarded as units exactly the same principle. Counties would be dealt with on exactly the same principle as boroughs, and every county and borough in England and Wales would be dealt with on identical lines with the counties and boroughs in Scotland and Ireland. The net result would be that England would obtain 6 additional seats, and Scotland 12 additional seats. No change would be made in the representation of Ireland, and Wales also would remain untouched. Next he dealt with the division of electoral areas, and stated that, as a general rule, the Bill would adopt (as a means, among other reasons, for securing variety of representation) the system of one-member districts, with a few exceptions, such as the City of London, and existing towns between 50,000 and 165,000 population, which would continue to be represented by 2 members. . . .[2]

(D) THE REDISTRIBUTION BILL

The Redistribution Bill framed by the leaders of both parties, and introduced by Mr. Gladstone on Monday in a clear, but unusually bold speech, has proved an almost unexpected success. It was never probable that such a Bill, accepted as a compromise by the two historic parties after a struggle of great severity, would be defeated or even gravely resisted, but there is literally no serious opposition. The Tories accept it without misgiving, the Liberals accept it with ardent hope; the Irish agree to its terms, though we may hear something of them in committee; and the crotchetteers, including the advocates of proportional representation, fold up their papers with a sigh, and with the exception of Mr. Courtney, who has resigned his post as Secretary to the Treasury, prepare to resign themselves to the inevitable. Even the disfranchised boroughs, greatly conciliated by giving their names to county districts, yield quietly to the national desire, and the only bitterness observable is in those boroughs which, electing at present two Members, are henceforward to return only one, and in some great towns which dislike subdivisions. . . .

This result is the more remarkable, and the more creditable to both leaders, because the Bill, besides being immensely wide, so wide as to amount, with its corollary, the Franchise Bill, to a pacific revolution, disturbs all personal interests in a way no previous Bill has ever done. With the exception of the sixty or so seats in boroughs with between 50,000 of population and 165,000, no seat in the country is unaffected. What with the disfranchisements, and the new franchise, and the increase in Members for large places, and the

[2]See also Appendix 4.

SOURCE. *The Economist* (December 6, 1884), p. 1474.

adoption throughout nine-tenths of the Kingdom of the one-member principle, every sitting Member will find himself, for one reason or another, addressing a new constituency. That is always unpleasant, even when the candidate is fairly hopeful of ultimate success, and is not afraid of the new committee, as well as constituency, to which he must address himself. For it must not be forgotten that, among other old things, most political organisations perish under the Bill. There will no longer be a Liverpool, but nine Liverpools, often singularly apart in feeling; no longer a Birmingham, but seven Birminghams, in one of which Lord Randolph Churchill hopes to find a seat. The county members will not only have to attract a new constituency, but to attract a new district, and to secure it without the concessions which the existence of the second Member often enabled him to make. He will rarely or never be unopposed, for the new Bribery Act makes elections comparatively cheap, and he will find that the local jealousies about him are greatly intensified by the reduction of his electoral area. The Members for little boroughs rarely live in them, the Members for little county districts do. So great, indeed, will be the disturbance, that we incline to believe the one-member principle the essence of the new Bill, and to discuss that rather than the slightly over-discussed gain to Democracy, or to the power of the Executive. . . .

7 The Significance of the Reform Acts of 1884–1885

(A) CHARLES SEYMOUR ON THE FRANCHISE ACT OF 1884

The failure of all attempts to extend the scope of the bill of 1884 left it imbued with the character that Gladstone had sought; it was as moderate as was consistent with the elimination of the chief anomalies that had characterized the suffrage since 1867.[1] The demands of the Conservatives for safeguards against the overwhelming force of numbers were indeed refused, or, at least, put off for later

SOURCE. Charles Seymour, *Electoral Reform in England and Wales, 1832–1885* (New Haven: Yale University Press, 1915), pp. 477–478, 480–482, 485–488. Reprinted by permission of the publisher.
[1] This was written in 1915 (ed.).

discussion. But the Radical attacks upon the existing barriers to democracy, upon the ancient property franchise, the town free-holder, the university elector, and the plural voter in all his forms—all such attacks failed absolutely. The basis of the suffrage since 1884 has thus failed to approach complete democracy. Old privileges and anomalies still remained, counteracting to some extent the newly won power of the masses in the counties.

The vestiges of the ancient electoral system, it is true, lost most of their influence in elections, and except in the counties have drawn forth but few complaints from the advocates of pure democracy. In the boroughs, after 1885, the ancient right voters numbered thirty-five thousand only, and were to be found in only fifty-six constituencies. In most of these boroughs the influence of the relics of the old system was negligible. At Taunton there were but four potwallers as reminder of the most picturesque of ancient franchises; in Westminster, the freemen who had once furnished inspiration to the genius of Hogarth, were represented by a single voter. And the loosely interpreted inhabitant franchise of Preston, which in the eighteenth century would have allowed a regiment quartered there overnight, to vote on the morrow, was accountable for only twenty-two electors. . . .

The fifteen years which followed the act of 1884 saw a slight decrease in the number of property owning electors, and by the end of the century their position in the electorate was becoming less and less important. In 1886 they formed twenty per cent of the county vote, in 1902 only sixteen per cent. And there were but twenty divisions where a quarter or more of the electors voted upon the ownership qualification.[2] Such a development was not unnatural, since the occupiers increased with the population, whereas the number of freeholders depended upon property and had approached its limit even in 1886.

No statistics are in existence showing without question what proportion of ownership electors possessed votes in more than one constituency. The number of plural voters has been estimated at close to half a million, which would mean that five-sixths of the owners were

---

[2]From 1886 to 1902 the ownership electors decreased from 508,000 to 493,000 in England and Wales. The occupation voters on the other hand increased from two millions to two millions and a half. In Stretford and in Wimbledon, Surrey, the ownership voters still formed, however, more than a third of the electorate, *Parliamentary Papers*, 1886, no. 44; 1902 no. 70.

plural voters. That a very large part of the ownership vote is an out-vote will probably not be questioned. It has also been asserted that eighty per cent of the plural voters are affiliated with the Conservatives. The accession of the Liberal Unionists, who had always controlled a large proportion of the town freeholder vote, doubtless transformed what had formerly been a factor of Conservative weakness into one of strength.

But in reality the ownership vote has probably affected Conservative strength in elections rather less than is popularly supposed. . . .

The great numerical increase consequent upon the Reform Act of 1884 is naturally to be found in the county occupation voters. The borough electorate was indeed reinforced by nearly two hundred thousand electors, but this gain of about eleven per cent resulted almost entirely from the enlargement of borough boundaries. In the counties the number of electors was nearly tripled, increasing from nine hundred thousand to two and a half millions. Proportionately the total increase of the electorate in 1884 was not so large as in 1867; but absolutely the number of new electors was nearly twice as great as at the time of the preceding reform.[3] . . .

The act of 1884 was the culmination of the process begun in 1832. The legislation of the latter year introduced the occupation franchise in both counties and boroughs, setting an arbitrary standard of value, and preserving the difference between the two kinds of constituencies by demanding a higher value in the counties. In 1867 the standard of value was not required in boroughs and that of the counties was lowered. In 1884 the process was logically completed by accepting as qualification in counties as in boroughs simply the occupation of a house. The next step, that which would involve absolute manhood

---

[3]The per cent increase in 1832 was 49; in 1867, 88; in 1884, 67. The per cent of increase in borough voters in 1867 was 134; of county voters in 1884, 162. Absolutely the reform of 1832 added 217,000 voters; that of 1867, 938,000; that of 1884, 1,762,000. After the reform of 1884 the electorate was made up as follows:

Occupation voters in boroughs	1,749,441
Occupation voters in counties	2,020,650
Ancient right voters in boroughs	35,066
Ownership voters in counties	508,554
Lodgers in boroughs	57,684
Lodgers in counties	8,937

Parliamentary Papers, 1886, no. 44.

suffrage, naturally belongs to a different epoch, and to a generation still more completely separated from the older electoral traditions.

The process which transformed the £10 and the £50 occupation franchises of 1832 into the household suffrage of the present day led, as we have seen, both to a change in the composition and to an increase in the size of the electorate. The act of 1832 was in its first effects by no means a democratic measure. A large proportion of the few labourers who had previously possessed the right to [of] vote were disfranchised; the new electors in boroughs, wherever they could vote independently, voted with narrow middle-class interests in view. And the new county electors were the tools of the landed aristocracy. Moreover the increase in the number of voters was small, partly because the franchises were themselves narrow, partly because of the restrictions of the registration system.

But the importance of the act of 1832, so far as it was concerned with voting rights, cannot be minimized. Besides opening up the close boroughs, a process which affected the balance of parties rather than of classes, it provided for an automatically increasing electorate, and in so doing sounded the knell of aristocracy. Before the Reform Act, the county electorate could not increase in proportion to the population, except by the creation of faggot votes; and the increase of the number of borough voters, under the ancient right franchises, was bound to a day when electoral anomalies were no longer defended on the ground of either prescriptive right or practical value. Theoretically the act of 1884 was merely the complement of that of 1867, although the importance of the results then achieved demands a far more dignified description.

It is at the same time an interesting and significant fact that the ancient right voter in boroughs, and the freeholder in counties still persisted after 1884. The anomaly of privilege, vested in the London liveryman, the freeman of Coventry, the plural-voting freeholder, or university voter, was not destroyed. A uniform doctrinaire principle of suffrage was not advanced in any of the three acts, nor was the franchise based in any respect upon the doctrine of the inmate voting rights of man.

Actually, however, the approach to manhood suffrage was so close, that the most progressive could afford to wait until the twentieth century before putting the franchise on a purely democratic basis. The reform in electioneering methods and the settlement of registration conditions accomplished in 1883 and 1885, went far, in combination with the new suffrage, towards completing the transfer of predominant political power from the aristocracy and middle classes to the nation as a whole. So far as the electoral aspect of the question was concerned, the process only demanded for its completion along broad lines, a thorough redistribution of seats. This was accomplished in 1885.

(B) CHARLES SEYMOUR ON THE REDISTRIBUTION ACT OF 1885

The failure to remove the anomaly of university representation, like the defeat of proportional representation, did not seriously affect the apathetic content with which the act, as passed, was received. The Radicals rejoiced in the disappearance of the small boroughs, and the Liberals congratulated themselves upon the favour shown the towns of moderate size; each party was naturally disappointed, however, that their special demands had not been more completely satisfied. The Conservatives regretted, on traditional grounds, the almost total disappearance of the numerous small constituencies in which property influence was strong, but they approved of the single-member districts and the concentration of power in the metropolis. At the same time the hard-shell Tories were by no means displeased at the partial survival of many numerical anomalies.

These anomalies became in a way more striking than before, since they were now the exception, whereas previously they had been the rule. Generally speaking the electoral advantages possessed by the southern and the agricultural constituencies disappeared in 1885. The industrial Northwest gained forty-eight seats and lost only eight, and the enormous accession of strength to the metropolis, forty-two members in all, has been noted. In the Southwest, on the other hand, thirty-three borough seats were disfranchised, so that even with the seven new county members there was a net loss of twenty-six seats. The southeastern group lost fourteen members, the south-midland lost eleven, and the west-midland ten. The counties of the southern seaboard, instead of returning half of the House of Commons as in unreformed days, were represented after 1885 by little more than a sixth.

SOURCE. Charles Seymour, *Electoral Reform in England and Wales, 1832–1885* (New Haven: Yale University Press, 1915), pp. 513–516. Reprinted by permission of the publisher.

The redistribution satisfied in broad lines, and for the moment, the Conservative contention that seats should be assigned according to population. This was especially true of the county divisions, where the ancient traditions were more generally disregarded and where a closer approximation to mathematical exactness was possible than in the boroughs. Not merely was the former electoral disadvantage of the counties removed, so that a county and a borough member represented on the general average the same number of inhabitants, but the ratio of seats to population was made regular throughout the county divisions. The average ratio for all England and Wales was one member to about every fifty-two thousand inhabitants. In the Northwest and the Southeast the ratio was slightly below the average, and in the East and Wales rather above it. But the proportional disadvantage of the concentrated centres of population and of industry as opposed to agriculture disappeared. In Middlesex, the south-midland, south-western, midland, and northern groups, whether of an urban or a rural character, the proportion of county members to population was practically the same. . . .

In the boroughs, however, while some of the industrial centres were given enough seats to raise their electoral power to a point not far from the average, the retention of the smaller boroughs of between fifteen and thirty thousand inhabitants, gave undue proportional weight to the districts in which they were situated. The proportion of borough members in the Southwest was twice that of the Midlands, and the towns of the southwestern group had also double the electoral strength of those in the Northwest in proportion to their population. But the anomalies which had worked to the disadvantage of the large commercial and manufacturing towns were at least diminished. The metropolitan group of boroughs, which had always been underrepresented, returned a member to every sixty-five thousand inhabitants; and the disadvantage of the industrial Northwest and Midlands was due not so much to their low ratio as to the high proportion in the southern boroughs. . . .

(C) THE THIRD REFORM ACT COMPARED TO THE ACTS OF 1832 AND 1867

We may also look at the extent to which the Third Reform Act was based on an accurate evaluation of the available evidence about the

SOURCE. Norman McCord, "Some Difficulties of Parliamentary Reform," in *Historical Journal*, Vol. X, pp. 387–390.

situation. Essentially the intention in the Third Reform Act was the same as its predecessors, that is to confer the franchise on those fitted for it by their character and attainments. By now, however, belief in the "improvement" of the lower classes had grown to such a degree that a very wide extent of enfranchisement could be conceived, if indeed not brought forth because of the technical weaknesses of the legislation already alluded to. Once again the reformers declared that their aim was to give the vote to those whose respectability and responsibility fitted them for the trust, but those virtues were now believed to be very widespread indeed. It was true that the 1867 settlement had shown itself to be imperfect and anomalous in practice, but the main force behind the reforming legislation of 1884–1885 was the Liberals' firm faith in the continuing and extensive improvement in the manners and the morals of the working classes. Once again, however, the reformers were willing to assume rose-coloured spectacles, and their belief in the respectability attained by the mass of the working classes by the mid-1880s was exaggerated. Throughout the second half of the nineteenth century optimism about this improvement ran ahead of the actual development, and again in the 1880s the reformers were conveniently avoiding a good deal of evidence which might have impugned their assumptions about the realities of working class life at the time. . . .

It may be justifiable then to regard all three of the nineteenth-century Reform Acts as "leaps in the dark," as none of them seems to have been based on any very accurate or extensive survey of the relevant facts of contemporary society, and all suffered from marked deficiencies in technical detail which prevented them from being more than very imperfect agents for effecting the changes aimed at.

One last point deserves to be made. If anyone wished to look anywhere for an excellent example of Britain "muddling through" to a tolerably satisfactory solution, the reform of Parliament is a good candidate, for the very difficulties considered above had a major part to play in smoothing the process. A question sometimes asked in examinations is whether in nineteenth-century Britain political reform kept pace with social and economic change. It may be that because these reforms were not closely related to objective assessments but much more to prevailing hopes and beliefs, that the happy optimism of the reformers played a valuable role in allowing parliamentary reform to anticipate social and economic change, and thereby to some extent to forestall serious strains in society and diminish their impact. Unlike modern Governments, the reformers had a good deal of freedom to act untrammelled by an immense array of inconvenient facts. Particularly in 1867 and 1884–1885, if the full import of the measures had been realized, the story of reform might have been much less smooth. Equally, if the reformers in these years had not been willing to adopt their rose-coloured spectacles the struggle for the transformation of Britain into a democracy might have been a great deal more bitter and prolonged. Perhaps the best example of this is that the electoral system so blithely created in 1884–1885 by the Gladstonian Liberals provided the framework for the creation and early successes of the Labour Representation Committee and the Labour party. After the Third Reform Act the working classes formed the majority of the electorate, however imperfect the system may have been. Political rights had been extended to large numbers of the workers at a time when their social and economic emancipation still had very far to go, a factor which perhaps contributed to the comparative ease and tranquillity which accompanied the rise of the working classes in the present century.

CONCLUSION

The Reform Acts of 1832, 1867, and 1884–1885 transformed the British parliamentary system from one which was aristocratic and oligarchic to one which was at least partially democratic. It is true that the system created by the Third Reform Act was still riddled with anomalies[1] and that a completely democratic system was not achieved until well into the twentieth century, but the real battle for democracy was over and the final instalments were introduced with remarkably little debate except for the female suffrage agitation in the years immediately preceding the First World War.[2] The landed aristocracy continued to play a major role in the governing of the country until the beginning of the twentieth century, but after each successive reform act it had to pay greater attention to the demands of voters from other classes. The failure to take sufficient cognizance of this point resulted in the formation of a Labour Party at the end of the century, which was responsible for the completion of the democratic system with its Representation of the People Act in 1948.

The largest, least controversial, and least written about of all the reform acts was that of 1918, passed by the Coalition Government of David Lloyd George (1863–1945), which enfranchised 8,000,000 voters. This measure gave the vote to all males over twenty-one years of age with six months residence (or occupation of business premises) and to all women over thirty who had six months ownership or tenancy of any land or premises or who were married to husbands so qualified. Female suffrage had divided both the Liberal and the Conservative parties in the years before 1914, but the social emancipation of women during the First World War, resulting from the part they played in it, brought general support for this first installment,

---

[1] See Neal Blewett, "The Franchise in the United Kingdom 1885–1918," *Past and Present*, No. 32 (1965), pp. 27–56.

[2] There had been zealous advocates of votes for women in the debates on the Second and Third Reform Acts, but their amendments had been defeated by large majorities.

which even passed the House of Lords by an almost two to one majority.[3] In 1928 the Conservative Government of Stanley Baldwin (1867–1947) completed the process with an act extending the vote to all women over twenty-one on the same terms as for men.[4]

The Reform Act of 1918 increased the membership of the House of Commons to 707, although this was reduced to 615 after the withdrawal of the Southern Irish members when the Irish Free State was separated from the United Kingdom in 1922. These seats were redistributed in equal electoral districts of approximately 70,000 population in Britain, exclusive of Ireland.[5] During the Second World War an all-party Speaker's Conference made recommendations leading to two bills: the Redistribution Act of 1944, which made a temporary addition of 25 seats to bring the total to 640; and the Representation of the People Act of 1945, which assimilated local and parliamentary franchises, reduced the business vote, and modified the registration machinery. A more important and controversial Representation of the People Act was passed in 1948, which provided for an extensive redistribution of seats, eliminated the university seats, and reduced the total number of seats to 625, a number subsequently raised to 630. This act also brought a final end to plural voting. Some of these provisions were attacked bitterly by the Conservative Opposition as breaking faith with the agreements of the wartime constitutional conference, but the act was passed without difficulty. Further acts consolidating the electoral laws were passed in 1949 without any controversy. The Conservatives promised to revive university representation, but they have not done so.

The history of electoral reform is in many respects a highly complex and technical subject and perhaps for this reason it has not received the full attention that it deserves from historians. Nevertheless it is an important part of the story of the emergence of a democratic system of government in Britain, which has had significance far

---

[3] *Annual Register 1918* (London, 1919), pp. 51–53. A separate bill, passed in the same year, allowed women for the first time to sit in the House of Commons (*ibid.*, p. 143).

[4] *Annual Register 1928* (London, 1929), pp. 33, 53. This added another five and a half million voters to the electorate [D. E. Butler, *The Electoral System in Britain 1918–1951* (Oxford, 1953) p. 33].

[5] The act also required all constituencies to go to the polls on the same day, considerably reduced the amount of allowed election expenses, and imposed a seat deposit forfeited by candidates failing to obtain one-eight of the votes cast (Butler, *Electoral System*, pp. 7–12).

beyond the British Isles. The economic, social, and political reasons behind the changes form some of the main threads of British history over the past two centuries, but in this collection of readings it has only been possible to examine them at the points of crisis that produced the major steps along the road from aristocratic to democratic government. In 1832 "democracy" was almost as pejorative a word as "communism" is today in many countries, but by 1885 a democratic suffrage was accepted as an accomplished fact by the classes who had once opposed it. Probably the majority of the members of both houses who gave their support to the second and third reform acts did so with some misgiving and uneasiness, conscious, as Lord Derby bluntly said, that they were "taking a leap in the dark", but reasonably confident that they and the country would "muddle through." Their faith has been sustained in that the democratic parliamentary cabinet system of government evolved in the nineteenth century has survived intact to this day, but they would not recognize the social system on which it now rests. That system probably would not have evolved as peacefully as it has were it not for the constitutional reforms of the nineteenth century. The passing of the Reform Acts of 1832, 1867, and 1884–1885 is an important chapter in British and in world history.

APPENDIX NO. 1[1]

THE ELECTORATE AND THE REFORMS IN ENGLAND AND WALES

	County Electorate	Borough Electorate	Total Electorate	Increase	% Increase
1831	247,000*	188,391*	435,391 ⎫		
1833	370,379	282,398	652,777 ⎬	217,386	49
1866	542,633	514,026	1,056,659 ⎫		
1869	791,916	1,203,170	1,995,086 ⎬	938,427	88
1883	966,721	1,651,732	2,618,453 ⎫		
1886	2,538,349	1,842,191	4,380,540 ⎬	1,762,087	67

*These figures obtained from an unpublished *Parliamentary Paper*, cited by John Lambert in "Parliamentary Franchises," *Nineteenth Century*, December, 1889. The county electorate is estimated. The form of the above table is the same as that published by Mr. Lambert, but his figures have been corrected from published *Parliamentary Papers*.

EFFECT OF REFORMS ON BOROUGH AND COUNTY ELECTORATES

		Increase	% Increase	Total Increase
1832	County	123,379	49 ⎫	
	Borough	94,007	49 ⎬	217,386
1867–1868	County	249,283	45 ⎫	
	Borough	689,144	134 ⎬	938,427
1884–1885	County	1,571,628	162 ⎫	
	Borough	190,459	11 ⎬	1,762,087

[1] From Charles Seymour, *Electoral Reform in England and Wales*, 1832–1885 (New Haven: Yale University Press, 1915), p. 533. Reprinted by permission of the publisher.

APPENDIX NO. 2[2]

ANALYSIS OF THE REDISTRIBUTION OF 1832

Disfranchisement Seats

55 double-seated boroughs absolutely disfranchised 110

 1 single-seated borough (Higham Ferrers) disfranchised 1

30 boroughs lose 1 seat apiece 30

Weymouth and Melcombe Regis lose 2 seats 2

 Total number of seats available 143

Enfranchisement

 26 counties divided 52

 10 counties receive 1 seat apiece 10

 Yorkshire receives 2 seats 2

 Isle of Wight separated from Hampshire 1

 22 large towns receive 2 seats apiece 44

 21 moderate-sized towns receive 1 seat apiece 21

 Total number of seats assigned 130

   4 seats given to Ireland
   8 seats given to Scotland
   1 seat given to Dublin University

[2]*Ibid.*, p. 538.

APPENDIX NO. 3[3]

ANALYSIS OF THE REDISTRIBUTION OF 1867–1868

Disfranchisement	*Seats*
3 double-seated boroughs disfranchised for corrupt practices	6
1 single-seated borough disfranchised for corrupt practices	1
3 double-seated boroughs (of less than 5000 population)	6
4 single-seated boroughs (of less than 5000 population)	4
35 boroughs lose 1 seat apiece	<u>35</u>
Total number of seats available	52

Enfranchisement	
10 counties redivided into 3 instead of 2 divisions	20
Lancashire receives 3 seats	3
Yorkshire West Riding receives 2 seats	2
Chelsea and Hackney receive 2 seats apiece	4
Liverpool, Birmingham, Manchester, Leeds, Salford, Merthyr Tydvil receive 1 seat apiece	6
9 moderate-sized towns receive 1 seat apiece	9
London University receives 1 seat	<u>1</u>
Total number of seats assigned	45

Scotland receives 7 seats

[3] *Ibid.*, p. 539.

APPENDIX NO. 4[4]

ANALYSIS OF THE REDISTRIBUTION OF 1885

Disfranchisement	*Seats*
7 double-seated boroughs (of less than 15,000 population)	14
65 single-seated boroughs (of less than 15,000 population)	65
6 double-seated boroughs (large rural constituencies)	12
2 corrupt double-seated boroughs	4
36 double-seated boroughs lose 1 seat apiece	36
City of London loses 2 members	2
Haverfordwest combined with Pembroke	1
Rutland and Herefordshire lose 1 seat apiece	2
Total number of seats available by disfranchisement	136
Seats available by raising numbers of House	2
Seats available by disfranchisement of Beverley and Bridgwater, 1870	4
Total number of seats available	142

Enfranchisement	
39 seats given to metropolitan boroughs	39
25 seats given to existing English boroughs	25
9 new provincial boroughs created in England	9
1 seat given to Swansea	1
64 seats given to English counties	64
4 seats given to Welsh counties	4
Total number of seats assigned	142

[4] *Ibid.*, p. 540.

SUGGESTIONS FOR FURTHER READING

(The original place of publication is London except where otherwise noted.)

GENERAL WORKS ON REFORM AND THE POLITICAL BACKGROUND

The standard work on the three Reform Acts is Charles Seymour, *Electoral Reform in England and Wales, 1832–1885* (Yale Historical Publications, New Haven, 1915). H. J. Hanham (ed.), *Nineteenth Century Constitution, 1815–1914: Documents and Commentary* (Cambridge, 1969) is the most recent documentary collection. W. C. Costin and J. S. Watson (eds.), *The Law and Working of the Constitution*, vol. II, 1784–1914 (1952) contains partial texts of the three acts. R. K. Webb, *Modern England from the Eighteenth Century to the Present* (New York, 1968) provides an admirable general background for the student unfamiliar with British history. Asa Briggs, *The Making of Modern England, 1783–1867: The Age of Improvement* (originally published in 1959 under the subtitle) has more detailed background of British history, 1783–1867, and excellent chapters on the First and Second Reform Acts.

THE REFORM ACT OF 1832

G. S. Veitch, *The Genesis of Parliamentary Reform* (1913) is the standard work on reform movements prior to 1832. For the immediate background see the Introduction to A. Aspinall (ed.), *Three Early Nineteenth Century Diaries* (1952). J. R. M. Butler, *The Passing of the Great Reform Bill* (1914) and G. M. Trevelyan, *Lord Grey of the Reform Bill* (1920) are two of the best-known books dealing with the passage of the First Reform Act; J. Hamburger, *James Mill and the Art of Revolution* (New Haven, 1963) is a more recent study of one aspect of the story. The subject is dealt with in many biographies and general histories, notably Chester New, *Lord Durham* (1929) and Élie Halévy, *A History of the English People in the Nineteenth Century*, vol. III, *The Triumph of Reform, 1830–1841* (1923, translated 1927), as well as other works quoted in the readings. The best modern interpretation is to be found in Norman Gash, *Politics in the age of Peel: A Study in the Technique of Parliamentary Representation 1830–1850* (1953).

THE REFORM ACT OF 1867

Two books have recently appeared on the Second Reform Act: F. B. Smith, *The Making of the Second Reform Bill* (Cambridge, 1966) is a painstaking and straightforward account rather from the Liberal point of view; Maurice Cowling, *Disraeli, Gladstone and Revolution: The Passing of the Second Reform Bill* (Cambridge, 1967) is much more involved and from the Conservative point of view. J. H. Park, *The English Reform Bill of 1867* is a more old-fashioned account, but still of some value. Of the many biographies that touch on the subject the most valuable are John Morley, *Life of Gladstone*, vol. II (1903), W. F. Monypenny and G. E. Buckle, *Life of Disraeli, Earl of Beaconsfield*, vol. IV (1916) or vol. II of the two-volume edition (New York, 1929), and Robert Blake, *Disraeli* (1967). See also F. Harrison, ed., *Essays on Reform* (1867) for the views of a number of Victorian intellectuals on the subject, the *Annual Register* for the years 1866 and 1867 for a detailed summary of the debate in and out of parliament, and G. E. Buckle (ed.), *Letters of Queen Victoria*, 2nd series, vol. I (1926) for relevant correspondence between the Queen and her ministers.

THE REFORM ACTS OF 1884–1885

There are no books specifically on these acts. Again the *Annual Register*, (for 1884 and 1885), *Letters of Queen Victoria* (2nd series, vol. III), and Morley's *Gladstone* (vol. III), are useful, as are other biographies as indicated in the readings. See also Agatha Ramm (ed.), *The Political Correspondence of Mr Gladstone and Lord Granville*, vol. II, *1883–1886* (Oxford, 1962). For the Reform Acts of the twentieth century see D. E. Butler, *The Electoral System in Britain 1918–1951* (Oxford, 1953).

ARTICLES

For a general article on the three acts see Norman McCord, "Some Difficulties of Parliamentary Reform," *Historical Journal*, vol. X (1967). For the Reform Act of 1832 see two articles by D. C. Moore, "The Other Face of Reform," *Victorian Studies*, vol. V (1961) and "Concession or Cure: the Sociological Premises of the First Reform Act," *Historical Journal*, vol. IX (1966). For the Reform Act of 1867 see two articles by F. H. Herrick, "The Reform Bill of 1867 and the British Party System," *Pacific Historical Review*, vol. III (1934) and "The Second Reform Movement in Britain," *Journal of the History of Ideas*, vol. IX (1948); also the essays by Royden Harrison and Gertrude Himmelfarb quoted in the readings. For the inadequacies of the Reform Acts of 1884–1885 see Neal Blewett, "The Franchise in the United Kingdom 1885–1918," *Past and Present*, no. 32 (1965). See also Corrine Comstock Weston, "The Royal Mediation in 1884," *English Historical Review*, vol. LXXXII (1967): and H. J. Hanham, *The Reformed Electoral System in Great Britain, 1832–1914*, Historical Association Pamphlet number 69 (London, 1968).